U.S. CIVIL WAR

BATTLE BY BATTLE

OSPREY
PUBLISHING

DEDICATION
TO SHARON VAN DER MERWE

U.S. CIVIL WAR

BATTLE BY BATTLE

IAIN MacGREGOR

OSPREY PUBLISHING
Bloomsbury Publishing Plc
Kemp House, Chawley Park, Cumnor Hill, Oxford OX2 9PH, UK
29 Earlsfort Terrace, Dublin 2, Ireland
1385 Broadway, 5th Floor, New York, NY 10018, USA
E-mail: info@ospreypublishing.com
www.ospreypublishing.com

OSPREY is a trademark of Osprey Publishing Ltd

First published in Great Britain in 2022

Artwork previously published in in the following Osprey titles: *Across a Deadly Field* (p. 24); CAM 52: *Gettysburg 1863* (p. 72); CAM 54: *Shiloh 1862* (p. 40); CAM 63: *Fredericksburg 1862* (p. 56); CAM 95: *Second Manassas 1862* (p. 48); CAM 133: *Seven Days Battles 1862* (p. 44); CAM 201: *Brandy Station 1863* (p. 68); CAM 267: *Wilderness and Spotsylvania 1864* (p. 92); CAM 279: *Appomattox 1865* (p. 124); CAM 290: *Atlanta 1864* (pp. 100, 112); CAM 295: *Chattanooga 1863* (p. 84); CAM 314: *Nashville 1864* (p. 116); CBT 2: *Union Infantryman vs Confederate Infantryman* (p. 12); CBT 12: *Confederate Cavalryman vs Union Cavalryman* (pp. 71, 115); CMD 7: *Robert E. Lee* (pp. 60, 74); DUE 14: *Confederate Ironclad vs Union Ironclad* (p. 32); ELI 62: *American Civil War Zouaves* (p. 106); ELI 73: *American Civil War Commanders (1)* (pp. 46, 58, 95, 127); ELI 89: *American Civil War Commanders (3)* (pp. 82, 122); ELI 94: *American Civil War Commanders (4)* (p. 118); FOR 6: *American Civil War Fortifications (1)* (p. 8); FOR 38: *American Civil War Fortifications (2)* (p. 104); MAA 170: *American Civil War Armies (1)* (p. 90); MAA 177: *American Civil War Armies (2)* (pp. 14, 102); MAA 179: *American Civil War Armies (3)* (p. 35); MAA 252: *Flags of the American Civil War (1)* (pp. 27, 55, 75, 99, 123); MAA 258: *Flags of the American Civil War (2)* (pp. 47, 51 left, 62, 87, 111); MAA 426: *The Confederate Army 1861–65 (2)* (p. 86); MAA 446: *The Confederate Army 1861–65 (6)* (p. 18); NVG 38: *American Civil War Artillery 1861–65 (1)* (p. 43); NVG 40: *American Civil War Artillery 1861–65 (2)* (pp. 11, 28, 107); NVG 49: *Mississippi River Gunboats of the American Civil War 1861–65* (p. 31); NVG 56: *Union River Ironclad 1861–65* (pp. 64, 67); WAR 6: *Confederate Infantryman 1861–65* (p. 126); WAR 13: *Union Cavalryman 1861–65* (pp. 91, 96, 98, 103, 108, 110); WAR 31: *Union Infantryman 1861–65* (pp. 23, 51 right, 52, 83); WAR 34: *Confederate Artilleryman 1861–65* (p. 16); WAR 54: *Confederate Cavalryman 1861–65* (pp. 36, 39, 119); WAR 114: *African American Soldier in the Civil War* (p. 78); WPN 10: *The Pattern 1853 Enfield Rifle* (p. 76); WPN 42: *Winchester Lever-Action Rifles* (p. 20); WPN 44: *The Flintlock Musket* (p. 80); WPN 56: *Sharpshooting Rifles of the American Civil War* (p. 120); and WPN 75: *Weapons of the Civil War Cavalryman* (p. 88).

A catalog record for this book is available from the British Library.

ISBN: PB 978 1 4728 5011 9;
eBook 978 1 4728 5009 6;
ePDF 978 1 4728 5008 9;
XML 978 1 4728 5010 2

22 23 24 25 26   10 9 8 7 6 5 4 3 2 1

Index by Mark Swift

Printed and bound in India by Replika Press Private Ltd.

Front cover: (Mark Stacey © Osprey Publishing)

Osprey Publishing supports the Woodland Trust, the UK's leading woodland conservation charity.

To find out more about our authors and books visit **www.ospreypublishing.com**. Here you will find extracts, author interviews, details of forthcoming events and the option to sign up for our newsletter.

MIX
Paper from responsible sources
FSC® C016779

CONTENTS

CHRONOLOGY

1861
April 12–13	Battle of Fort Sumter
July 21	Battle of First Manassas/First Bull Run
August 10	Battle of Wilson's Creek/Oak Hills, Missouri
September 13–20	Battle of First Lexington
October 21	Battle of Ball's Bluff/Leesburg

1862
February 11–16	Battle of Fort Donelson, Tennessee
March 7–8	Battle of Pea Ridge/Elkhorn Tavern, Arkansas
March 8–9	Naval Battle of Hampton Roads
March 26–28	Battle of Glorieta Pass
April 6–7	Battle of Shiloh
May 8	"Stonewall" Jackson wins the Battle of McDowell; other victories follow at Front Royal (May 23), First Winchester (May 25), Cross Keys (June 8), and Port Republic (June 9)
May 31–June 1	Battle of Seven Pines/Fair Oaks
June 25–July 1	Seven Days battles reverse a tide of Union military success. Mechanicsville (June 26), Gaines' Mill (June 27), Savage's Station (June 29), Glendale/Frayser's Farm (June 30), and Malvern Hill (July 1)
August 9	Battle of Cedar Mountain
August 29–30	Battle of Second Manassas/Second Bull Run
September 17	Battle of Antietam/Sharpsburg
December 13	Battle of Fredericksburg
December 31–Jan 2	Battle of Murfreesboro/Stone's River, Tennessee

1863
April 30–May 6	Battle of Chancellorsville
May 18–July 4	Siege of Vicksburg, Mississippi
July 10–11	First Battle of Fort Wagner
June 9	Cavalry battle at Brandy Station
June 14–15	Second Battle of Winchester
July 1–3	Battle of Gettysburg
July 18	Second Battle of Fort Wagner
September 19	Battle of Chickamauga, Tennessee, begins
September 23	Bragg lays siege to Chattanooga
November 24	Hooker drives Confederates off Lookout Mountain
November 25	Sherman's attack stalls; Thomas' men storm Missionary Ridge

1864

February 22	Battle of Okolona
March 12	Grant is commissioned lieutenant-general and general-in-chief, to command all Federal armies. Halleck becomes chief of staff
March 18	Sherman assumes command of Union forces in the west
May 5–7	Battle of the Wilderness
May 6	Sherman opens Atlanta campaign
May 8–21	Battle of Spotsylvania Court House
May 11	Battle of Yellow Tavern; Gen. J.E.B. Stuart is mortally wounded and dies the next day
May 15	Battle of New Market
May 23–27	Battle of the North Anna River
May 31–June 12	Battle of Cold Harbor
June 5	Battle of Piedmont
June 15–18	Opening engagements around Petersburg
June 27	Sherman's assault on Kennesaw Mountain repulsed
July 9	Battle of Monocacy
July 22	Battle of Atlanta
July 24	Second Battle of Kernstown
July 30	Dramatic explosion of mine at Petersburg turns into the Battle of the Crater
August 31	Battle of Jonesborough, Georgia
September 1	Battle of Jonesborough concluded; Hood evacuates Atlanta
September 2	Sherman occupies Atlanta
September 19	Third Battle of Winchester
September 22	Battle of Fisher's Hill
October 19	Battle of Cedar Creek
November 15	Sherman's troops burn Atlanta; begin March to the Sea
December 15–16	Battle of Nashville
December 21	Sherman occupies Savannah

1865

February 5–7	Battle of Hatcher's Run
March 19–21	Sherman repulses Johnston's attack at Bentonville, North Carolina
March 29–31	The final campaign in Virginia begins with fighting around the Dinwiddie Court House
April 1	Battle of Five Forks
April 9	Lee surrenders to Grant at Appomattox Court House
April 13	Raleigh falls to Sherman
May 13	Last battle of the war, at Palmito Ranch, Texas

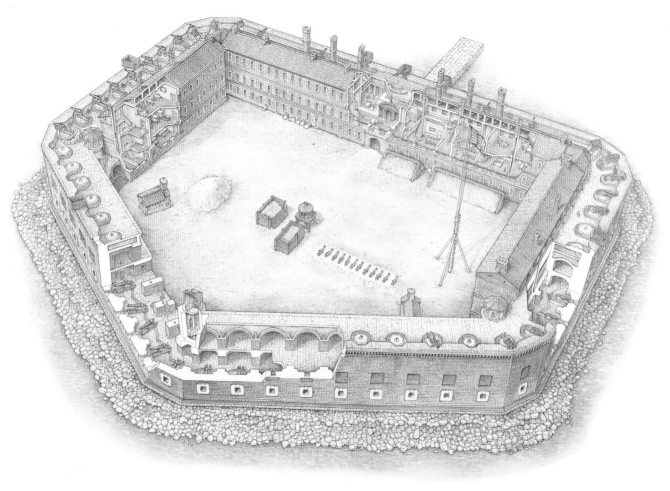

THE BATTLE OF FORT SUMTER
April 12–13, 1861

Slavery would be the primary political issue that brought on the Civil War of 1861–65 in the United States of America. By the spring of 1861, the presidency had been decided, with the Republican and pro-abolitionist Abraham Lincoln winning by a landslide. By this point the battle lines between those cotton-producing states wishing to secede to form the Confederate States of America (CSA) and those that remained loyal to the Union were firmly in place. Fearful of their cotton-producing economies being compromised by the freeing of the 4 million slaves they required to sustain it, the 11 slave-owning states would ratify secession, a move precipitated by South Carolina on December 20, 1860 and soon followed by Mississippi, Florida, Alabama, Georgia, Louisiana, and Texas; by the summer, Virginia, Arkansas, North Carolina, and Tennessee would follow, with both Kentucky and Missouri joining later that year but not officially ratified through their respective legislatures.

The pressure for the South to act and seize all Federal property within their borders and acquire the arsenals with which to arm their own hastily formed militias intensified. South Carolina's state legislature now looked upon the Federal fortifications which controlled access in and out of Charleston Harbor, the state's largest city. By April 1861, Lincoln had rejected any Confederate overtures for a peace treaty, citing them as an illegitimate government, only stoking greater tension as calls raged across the South to eject all Federal military, civilian, and judicial elements from their territory.

LEFT Fort Sumter, built to protect the port of Charleston, South Carolina, is best known for the role it played at the start of the Civil War. (Donato Spedaliere © Osprey Publishing)

Fort Sumter was a formidable gun platform that dominated the entrance in and out of Charleston Harbor and was used as the headquarters of the local Federal forces in the city. Appointed in February, its new commander—Maj. Robert Anderson of the 1st U.S. Artillery Regiment, a native Kentuckian—now faced off against Maj. Gen. P.G.T. Beauregard whom he had himself taught at West Point Military Academy. Anderson assessed that his small force of 85 men was best placed to defend Federal interests by evacuating their landward bases around the harbor to the safety of Fort Sumter. The Confederates quickly decided to lay siege, redirecting their batteries to best threaten the fort, as well as cut off resupply.

The siege became the first crisis of Lincoln's new administration. The standoff became ever more aggressive as the rebellion developed, with the formation of the Confederacy and Jefferson Davis proclaimed as its first president. With Maj. Anderson informing Washington his rations were running low, Lincoln ordered supply ships to sail south to his aid and notified the city's authorities of their arrival, the watching civilian population and press wondering who would fire first.

On April 9, Beauregard was instructed by President Davis to issue an ultimatum for the garrison's surrender or else it would be taken by force. Aware of his precarious position—outnumbered and heavily outgunned—Anderson chose to decline the ultimatum, bidding Beauregard's aide goodbye with the fateful words, "If we never meet in this world again, God grant that we may meet in the next." The rebel bombardment began at 4:30am on April 12 as 43 guns and mortars shelled the fort continuously for 34 hours. Anderson insured none of his men were exposed to the deadly salvoes as they returned fire from the fort's protected lower levels. The wooden outbuildings were now aflame and the masonry superstructure partially destroyed, but no federal casualties had been suffered.

RIGHT The 8-inch columbiad, a standard fortification cannon, fired a 32-pound shot and required seven or eight men to fire. (Tony Bryan © Osprey Publishing)

Into the second day, his men exhausted and hungry, and with no immediate relief in sight, Anderson agreed to surrender the fort at 2:30pm that day. As the garrison sailed back across the harbor into captivity, a 100-gun salute to their gallantry accidentally ignited a pile of cartridges in the fort which exploded, killing two privates standing nearby—the first fatalities of the war. Anderson would keep the fort's flag he had lowered and return it to Washington where it became a symbol of Union fortitude to return the rebel states to the nation.

Following Sumter's capitulation, Lincoln issued a proclamation for a volunteer 90-day army of 75,000 men he would send down to the South to recapture all Federal properties the rebels were now in control of. Perhaps his government underestimated the extent of support that existed for the Confederacy among its population; in any event, the Civil War had now begun in earnest. As a poignant footnote, the first unit from South Carolina to be mustered into the Confederate Army was the 1st South Carolina Rifles. Of the 1,500 men who served in its ranks, only 157 would remain by war's end.

THE BATTLE OF FIRST MANASSAS/ FIRST BULL RUN

July 21, 1861

Only three months after the surrender of Fort Sumter at Charleston, President Lincoln's proclamation for his 90-day army to suppress secessionism had raised over 75,000 troops but served to quickly push four more wavering states toward the Confederacy. With the secession of Virginia, Richmond now became the Confederate capital, a mere 100 miles away from Washington.

The Union had a population of over 18 million citizens. In terms of fighting manpower, Lincoln could call upon almost three times as many men to serve as the South. The continent's heavy industry and manufacturing centers were based in the North, too, as was two-thirds of the country's railway network, making supply to its troops in the field and its ability to outmaneuver the South even greater. Finally, the North commanded practically all the naval vessels currently in use; thus, a successful blockade of the South would be put into action.

For the South, buoyed by the perceived righteousness of their cause, the coming conflict would establish their right to be internationally recognized. Both sides had no concept of how bloody and long the coming war was to be. At Manassas Railway Junction, 25 miles outside of Washington, their two citizen armies, led by inexperienced commanders, would clash for the first time on a warm July day.

LEFT The men of the 33rd Virginia charge down Henry House Hill towards the position of the 11th New York. (Peter Dennis © Osprey Publishing)

The South was to be led by the "Hero of Fort Sumter" Brig. Gen. P.G.T. Beauregard, a proud Louisianan, and supported by a Virginian, Lt. Gen. Joseph Johnston, a veteran of West Point and the Mexican–American War. He was ordered by President Davis and his chief military adviser, Gen. Robert E. Lee, to move north toward Manassas junction—where Southern spies in Washington had forewarned them the Union Army was heading—to capture it before launching an offensive on Richmond. Once there and constructing defensive positions, Beauregard sent urgent orders for Johnston, situated 34 miles away in the Shenandoah Valley, to join him via train transport as quickly as possible. He commanded two

corps totaling 32,000 men, supported by an artillery wing, and a regiment of Virginian cavalry led by the brash young commander Col. J.E.B. Stuart.

Union forces were led by Brig. Gen. Irvin McDowell, a 42-year-old U.S. Army officer, who many feared had been promoted above his ability. He advanced toward Manassas but then vacillated for two days, deliberating his next steps. In support was the aging Maj. Gen. Robert Patterson, whose role had been to shadow Joseph Johnston's army, thought to be in the Shenandoah Valley. The Union army was a formidable force of infantry, totaling 35,000 men within five divisions, though supported by fewer artillery and less experienced cavalry than the Confederates.

On the morning of July 21, the Confederate positions stretched 6 miles along Bull Run Creek, protecting their vital rail junction at Manassas. Half of Johnston's men were by now almost in place, with the remainder on their way to the battlefield. Both sides had planned to attack their enemy's left flank, but it was the Union forces which struck first. The day's intense fighting would progress in two distinct phases as superior Union forces in the morning drove the Confederates from their positions at Bull Run Creek and Matthews Hill and back toward their final line at Henry House Hill. To Union troops and civilian onlookers it seemed they had almost won the day, with one more push at the rebel center bringing victory.

By lunchtime, however, Johnston's final units had arrived to bolster the Confederate defense, including the 1st Virginian Brigade commanded by Brig. Gen. Thomas J. Jackson, supported with artillery and cavalry. As Confederates fell back from the Union advance, who now held a 2-to-1 numerical advantage, Jackson's brigade took up a defensive line behind Henry House Hill to meet the Union advance. Confederate artillery silenced their counterparts as the discipline of Jackson's brigade awaiting the fight galvanized nearby retreating Southerners. The Virginians rose to unleash a withering fire on McDowell's men, who broke as the Southerners then charged them with bayonets drawn and uttering the "rebel yell" (a wild scream roared as the Confederate soldier advanced) for the first time in battle.

The Confederate right flank was now reinforced by Beauregard, as along the whole line the Union troops fell back, which quickly turned into a rout as Federal troops flung their weapons aside and ran for dear life, followed by dozens of Washington civilians who had come for a day out to watch a Union victory. For days afterwards, demoralized troops staggered into the capital and the country realized it was going to take more than one battle to win this war.

LEFT This Union colonel of infantry in 1861 wears the field-grade officer's full dress, with dress hat, frock coat, and dark trousers. (Ron Volstad © Osprey Publishing)

THE BATTLE OF WILSON'S CREEK/ OAK HILLS

August 10, 1861

Often labelled the "Bull Run of the West" and less well known though fought only 20 days later, this would be the first major battle between Union and Confederate forces west of the Mississippi River as both sides sought to gain dominance over the state of Missouri. Admitted into the Union in 1821, the slave-owning state had been at the heart of the abolitionist versus slave-owning debate for years, which had led to open conflict between armed groups from both sides from 1856 until the beginning of the Civil War. The German and Irish immigrants who settled in northern Missouri brought with them a strong tie to the Union and for the abolition of slavery. The state's agrarian economy was still reliant on slavery, and slaves themselves still made up 10 percent of the state's population by the beginning of the war.

As the call to armed conflict grew louder in the spring of 1861 across the Southern states, the state legislature of Missouri was adamant they wished to stay neutral, and a convention held in February had concluded the state would not secede from the Union. Neither would they give up slavery, nor supply soldiers and supplies of arms to either side. While commendable, this middle path brought with it conflict due to Missouri's strategic importance for both sides. Whoever controlled the Mississippi River, and the key city of St. Louis that guarded it, would thus dominate the western theater.

LEFT Union troops attack Confederate positions as the cannoneers attempt to remove their piece by prolongue. (Bill Younghusband © Osprey Publishing)

A key figure who would bring the state into the war was the Missouri state governor and secessionist Claiborne Fox Jackson. In secret communications with Confederate President Jefferson Davis, he wished to force the issue of making Missouri secede from the Union and made plans to seize St. Louis and capture its federal arsenal with militia units he had been raising in the slave-owning areas of the state. The plan was nipped in the bud through the quick actions of the federal arsenal's commander, Captain Nathaniel Lyon.

Tensions continued to build as the country broke apart. Jackson succeeded in the state's militia being recognized as the Missouri State Guard with a Confederate sympathizer, Stirling Price, commanding it. With Jackson now openly recruiting for the

Confederacy and Union loyalists being targeted by the militias, the Union Army took the step of promoting Lyon to brigadier general and in charge of the Department of the West, which oversaw the command federal troops west of the Mississippi River to the coast of California and Oregon. Throughout June and July open conflict resulted in skirmishes across the state.

By August, Jackson had been sacked as governor by the Missouri State Convention, and a 12,000-strong Confederate force led by Brig. Gen. Benjamin McCullough had invaded the state. Encamped at Springfield and with only 5,000 troops at his disposal—a mixture of militia and regular forces—Brig. Gen. Lyon decided he had to attack the rebels encamped at Wilson's Creek some 10 miles away to the southwest, or else give up southern Missouri to the

Confederacy. He then divided his command further, with 1,200 men led by Col. Franz Siegel to advance quickly and come up around and behind the Confederate camp, while his main force would drive the rebels from the high ground overlooking Wilson's Creek, thus either destroying them where they stood, or driving them from Missouri altogether.

At dawn on August 10, with no Confederate pickets set out to detect their movements, the Federals enjoyed early successes from the south as Siegel's artillery barrage panicked the rebel camp, driving off their cavalry, while Lyon's men to the north advanced to take the high ground, a vantage point later named "Bloody Hill." Counter-battery fire from the Arkansas state militia saved a Confederate rout and forced Lyon's men onto the defensive. Meanwhile, Siegel's force suffered disaster as an enemy formation—the 3rd Louisiana—was mistaken as Federal reinforcements (the 1st Iowa), who attacked his flank at close range, causing heavy casualties and forcing the Federals to retreat in confusion.

Lyon was now left alone to hold off multiple attacks by a superior force as they attempted to storm his position on "Bloody Hill." Leading a futile counterattack, Lyon was killed with a shot through his heart, the first general officer to die in combat in the Civil War. Eyeing the now precarious Federal position, Lyon's replacement, Maj. Samuel D. Sturgis, gave the order to retreat. After six hours of fierce fighting, the Confederates were in no shape to pursue, having suffered just as many casualties, allowing Sturgis to eventually stagger back to the fortifications of Rolla, 110 miles to the northeast. The Confederates, though, now held a rump of southern Missouri, which would ultimately announce secession from the Union that autumn.

LEFT An enlisted man of the Moniteau County Rangers, a Confederate unit which fought at the Battle of Wilson's Creek. (Richard Hook © Osprey Publishing)

THE BATTLE OF FIRST LEXINGTON
September 13–20, 1861

This was a small-scale battle in terms of the size of the units involved, but from a localized viewpoint was strategically important as to whether the Confederates or the Unionists could control the whole state of Missouri, and with it, the Missouri and Mississippi rivers. Following the victory by Confederate forces at Wilson's Creek the previous month, the Missouri State Guard portion of the rebel army now turned its attention to the small towns close to the Missouri–Kansas border in order to prevent incursions by pro-Union units of Kansas militia. Located on a pivotal position on the Missouri River, Lexington was an agricultural-based town with a population of 4,000 in the western-central part of the state. Many of its inhabitants were slave owners (over 30 percent of the town's population comprised slaves).

Union troops had previously taken up defensive positions in the town that summer as a precaution, but then relocated back to St. Louis due to their 90-day enlistment expiring. By the second week of September, the town was garrisoning a battalion of U.S. Reserves, who had subsequently been reinforced by the 23rd Illinois Volunteer Infantry, arriving just prior to the commencement of hostilities. The commander of the Union forces was Col. James A. Mulligan, a New Yorker, who had scant forces with which to defend the town and prevent the Missouri State Guard from obtaining any cash remaining in the Lexington bank—it held close to a million dollars which he was under orders to impound.

Claiborne Fox Jackson was still just as keen to obtain the much-needed cash in order to fund his pro-Confederate militia with which he planned to drive

LEFT A group of Union soldiers armed with Henry rifles takes a heavy toll on attacking Confederate infantry armed with standard rifle-muskets. (Mark Stacey © Osprey Publishing)

the state into secession, even though the legislature had voted against it. Their commander, Maj. Gen. Stirling Price, mirrored Governor Jackson's intentions, his force now numbering 15,000 men, far superior to the smaller Yankee force holding the town, even if the latter were better trained, armed, and supplied.

Col. Mulligan had set his men to work on constructing defensive positions around College Hill and taking over the Masonic College as his headquarters, giving a good field of fire for the coming attack. He was soon reinforced by men from the loyal 13th Missouri Infantry, swelling his garrison to 3,500 men—just in time, as the rebel militia soon cut the town off. Price and his force now camped outside the town, making plans to send in skirmishers the next morning to assess Mulligan's positions.

The fighting the next day was sporadic as Price's militia cavalry tried to charge the barriers surrounding the hill but were driven back by fire from two companies of Federals. Price then ordered a tactical withdrawal to await infantry and artillery which got into position that afternoon to launch an assault. Coming from the south of town along the main road into Lexington, the rebel militia charged six companies of Union troops who were forced back by sheer weight of numbers. The Union line around the college now came under artillery bombardment, which subsided once the rebels had run out of ammunition.

His men exhausted from the fighting, Price ordered a withdrawal several miles to the south of town, bivouacking on Lexington fairground. At a Union council of war, many officers expressed the opinion to abandon their position, but Mulligan refused, ordering them to hold out for as long as possible in the vain hope of reinforcement.

On the morning of September 18, the next rebel assault went in, Price determined to capture a key fortification on the perimeter called the Anderson House: a three-story building being used as a hospital. Despite a Union counterattack, Price's men finally occupied the building and established a firing platform.

Mulligan's position became more tenuous when his only water supply at a nearby creek was blocked by his besiegers. Although well-armed and provisioned for a

lengthy siege, without water they were doomed to defeat as the rebels tightened the ring around the college grounds. On the 20th, another assault drove the Union troops back further into the fortifications, only stopped by the confusion of a white flag flown by one of Mulligan's officers. Caught by surprise and unwilling to give in, he was pressured by Price to seek the opinion of his subordinates who voted in favor to capitulate by six to two. Reluctantly, Mulligan accepted Price's terms of unconditional surrender, handing over his garrison's valuable supplies and the money he was guarding. Though his men were paroled, Mulligan refused, was imprisoned and later swapped in a prisoner exchange, thus allowing him to fight on in the war. He was killed in action campaigning in Virginia in 1864.

ABOVE The M1861 .58-caliber rifled musket emerged as the weapon of choice for many Union foot soldiers. (John White © Osprey Publishing)

THE BATTLE OF BALL'S BLUFF/ LEESBURG

October 21, 1861

Three months had passed since the Union debacle at First Bull Run, and the Army of the Potomac—as it was now titled—had a new commander in the shape of Maj. Gen. George B. McClellan, an ambitious, highly organized, and able administrator. He had quickly rebuilt the shattered army that had run back to Washington into a formidable, well-trained, and well-supplied force, now capable of marching down to the Virginia peninsula to take on and defeat the Confederates. That was the plan McClellan had outlined to President Lincoln and his Secretary of War, Edwin McMasters Stanton.

LEFT Col. Charles Devens' command lost 449 killed or wounded and over 500 captured at the Battle of Ball's Bluff. (Mark Stacey © Osprey Publishing)

Amid the planning, and as both sides faced one another across the Potomac River, the Confederate commander in the field, Mississippian Col. Nathan Evans, unaware of McClellan's plan, became concerned at the buildup of Federal troops in the area. With little more than 3,000 fellow Mississippians in his brigade, he rightly feared the enemy to his front would also then try to turn his flank further upstream. This worry became very real when a skirmish developed nearby at Harpers Ferry on October 16, confirming Evans' fears as he then ordered his brigade to pull back from their defensive positions at Leesburg.

On the opposite bank, Brig. Gen. Charles P. Stone was commanding a corps of observation tasked with monitoring enemy movements and duly reported the withdrawal to McClellan's headquarters. On October

19, McClellan ordered Brig. Gen. George A. McCall to march his division to the town of Dranesville, 12 miles south of Leesburg, to ascertain what the rebels were up to. Unbeknownst to both men, on the same day Evans had now returned to Leesburg after being ordered by his commanding officer, Brig. Gen. P.G.T. Beauregard, back to defensive positions outside of the town.

On October 20, McClellan himself visited Dranesville to discuss matters in person and ordered Brig. Gen. Stone to send a small unit across the river to gauge Confederate response and strength. Stone directed troops to Edwards Ferry; some crossed over to the Virginia shoreline and returned, he strengthened defensive works along the river and even ordered battery fire into suspected Confederate positions—all without any reaction from the enemy. Curious for more news, Stone then ordered a reconnaissance party, which brought back mistaken sightings of a Confederate camp in the woods, forcing him to follow this up with what was a larger raiding party of 300 men of the 15th Massachusetts led by Col. Charles Devens.

The following morning, October 21, events soon overtook any functioning plan of action. Told no rebel camp existed by Col. Devens, Stone ordered reinforcements across and ordered Devens to strike deeper toward Leesburg. Attending his headquarters was United States Senator (and Colonel) Edward Dickinson Baker, who had set out to see for himself what was going on. Briefed by Stone, he was ordered to go to the crossing and decide whether Devens needed further reinforcements or should withdraw back across the river.

On his way to the river, Baker was met by a messenger from Devens with a dispatch reporting the Union commander's encounter with superior enemy forces from the 17th Mississippi and urging for reinforcements to cross the river to his aid. With hardly any boats in the vicinity, a bottleneck had developed, leaving many federal troops waiting on the opposite shore. At the frontline, Devens' position came under increasing pressure as yet more Confederates appeared to attack. With little option, he ordered a withdrawal back to the river at 2:30pm and finally met with Baker, who had now gotten across the Rappahannock just before a heavy Confederate attack came on them. After two more hours of a staggered retreat, Baker was shot and killed as the fighting grew in intensity.

It was as the darkness closed in that a fresh Confederate regiment launched the final assault. Scrambling for dear life, Devens' men ran down to the steep slopes of Ball's Bluff to find protection and escape the enemy fire. Some took their chances swimming back across the river despite the cold, while others crammed into what boats were available, resulting in many capsizing and the wounded drowning. Days later, Federal pickets as far away as Washington itself would discover their bloated bodies floating to shore.

Although not a major engagement, Devens' command lost 449 killed or wounded and over 500 captured, and the death of Senator Baker would have repercussions for the rest of the war. Members of the U.S. Congress became concerned at the many military reversals in the first year of the war and debated furiously as to whether the Union cause was being betrayed from within. As a fallout, the Congressional Joint Committee on the Conduct of the War was established, and primarily used by generals serving in Washington as a talking shop to enhance their chances of promotion to senior command.

RIGHT Flag presented to the 8th Virginia Infantry Regiment by Brig. Gen. Beauregard in recognition of valor in the Battle of Ball's Bluff. (Rick Scollins © Osprey Publishing)

THE BATTLE OF FORT DONELSON

February 11–16, 1862

While the Army of the Potomac was marooned outside Richmond in the east, the western theater proved more successful for the Union's strategic plans. In order to gain the upper hand in Kentucky and Tennessee, which would then serve as a platform for a future invasion of the South, the forts guarding the Cumberland and Tennessee rivers had to be taken. The task was given to an ex-U.S. Army regular who had been—up until the outbreak of the war a year before—a lowly clerk in Galena, Illinois: Brig. Gen. Ulysses S. Grant.

To capture the forts, Grant would initially have 25,000 men under his command—the Army of the Tennessee—supported with artillery fire from gunboats of the Western Gunboat Flotilla, commanded by Flag Officer Andrew H. Foote. Grant's capture of Fort Henry on February 6 had been relatively smooth, allowing Union access into the Tennessee River. Many of Fort Henry's garrison, however, had fled to the relative safety of Fort Donelson 10 miles away to bolster its defenses.

Fort Donelson dominated the Cumberland River, garrisoned by 16,000 men of the Army of Central Kentucky and led by Brig. Gen. John B. Floyd—who had served as the U.S. Secretary of War before 1861. Grant quickly set about cutting all supply links to Donelson, stationing the troops at his disposal at the fort's key entry and exit points. The fort, he knew, would be a tough nut to crack, with high walls, better entrenchments, and much greater firepower from the various batteries stationed within it, which enjoyed deadly fields of fire both on the water and landward sides. February 13, amid the wintry conditions now

LEFT Vicksburg, sitting on high bluffs overlooking the Mississippi, was a natural place for the Confederates to defend their control of the river. (Tony Bryan © Osprey Publishing)

setting in, saw various Union probes to spot weaknesses in the rebel lines repulsed with light casualties.

Aware of their precarious situation and with no news of reinforcements, the Confederate command decided to break out, not realizing 10,000 fresh Union troops had arrived that evening from Fort Henry, supported by six naval gunboats. Brig. Gen. Floyd was in reality a civilian and had handed over command to his subordinate, Brig. Gen. Gideon J. Pillow, who would command the breakout the following day. Unfortunately, Pillow's nerve was shot, and as the breakout began, he called the operation off, much to the disgust of his officers who recognized their fleeting chance of escape had now evaporated.

At dawn on the 15th, the Confederates tried once more to break out, with Pillow launching a major attack on the landward side to push the Union lines open and thus make the road to Nashville tenable. The initial first hours brought success as the stunned Union troops fell back, panicked by the onrushing rebels, yelling furiously as they charged into the fight. The infantry was supported by the Confederate cavalry attacking the Union flank, led by Col. Nathan Bedford Forrest, later a legend of the South.

Initially caught by surprise, Grant rushed into action, commanding a belligerent defense to hold the rebels from pushing any further. Pillow again lost his nerve at the crucial moment, ordering a retreat to the safety of the fortifications, but Union brigades quickly followed and seized their outer earthworks. It seemed now only a matter of time before further assaults would take the fort itself.

A midnight Confederate council of war concluded further fighting would result in fearful casualties, while a wholesale escape would be impossible, so the option to surrender had to be taken. Despite this, both Floyd and Pillow—fearful of how their reputations in the North might affect their treatment—decided upon flight, leaving a junior officer (Brig. Gen. Simon Bolivar Buckner) to oversee the surrender later that day. A disgusted Nathan Bedford Forrest refuted the plan, stating, "I did not come here to surrender my command," and led his 800 men through Federal lines and on a 70-mile horse ride through the frozen countryside back to Southern lines.

Grant refused any Southern terms offered other than unconditional surrender. Buckner, faced with certain defeat, accepted the inevitable, and 12,500 Confederates, with 48 artillery pieces and valuable supplies which Grant now took, marched into captivity. Amid the bad news from Virginia, Grant's capture of Forts Henry and Donelson gave the Union the shot in the arm it needed and catapulted him into the public's gaze. The legend of "Unconditional Surrender" Grant had begun.

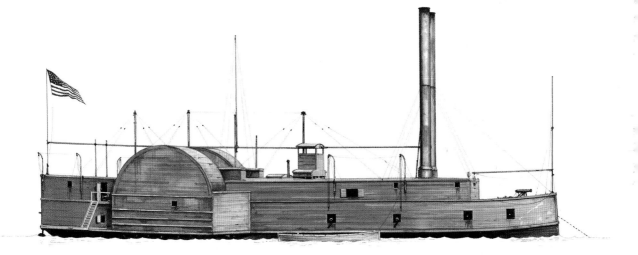

ABOVE The USS *Lexington* provided gunfire support for the Union Army at the battle. (Tony Bryan © Osprey Publishing)

THE NAVAL BATTLE OF HAMPTON ROADS

March 8–9, 1862

The strategy of strangling all routes of supply in and out of Confederate territory—known as the "Anaconda Plan"—was steadily succeeding. The Federal armies in the western theater had begun to capture key strategic points along the Mississippi, Tennessee, and Cumberland rivers, while along the eastern coast, the U.S. Navy were blocking all rebel shipping routes. The vital port of Charleston Harbor in South Carolina, and the shipping routes out of Richmond were now impossible for Confederate ships to navigate safely unless a solution to the North's monopoly on sea power could be broken.

LEFT The CSS *Virginia* shudders from the impact as shells from guns of the CSA *Monitor* strike her stern during the Battle of Hampton Roads. (Howard Gerrard © Osprey Publishing)

The Secretary of the Confederate Navy, Stephen R. Mallory, had envisaged such a scenario and led discussions for the construction of a metal-hulled, heavily armed vessel that would be impervious to enemy cannon fire and capable of getting into close-quarter combat to sink enemy ships. Southern engineers concluded no iron works were big enough to construct the steam engines and screw propellers required to power such a ship, but a solution was to be found in the burnt-out hulk of the USS *Merrimac*, a 275-foot-long vessel that had been abandoned by Union forces at the Gosport Navy Yard, in Portsmouth, Virginia, in 1861. The port's dry docks were still intact, as was the armory, thus handing over all the tools required to build the Civil War's first ironclad. Commissioned in February 1862 as the CSS *Virginia*, she was protected by two layers of 50mm-thick heavy iron plate, armed with an iron ram lifted at her prow, plus a formidable range of ten heavy guns capable of piercing 8 inches of plate armor, and with a crew of 352.

Well aware of the South's intentions, the North set up a commission under Secretary of the Navy Gideon Welles to ascertain the best design to be built, with the winner coming from the brilliant Swedish inventor John Erricson. The USS *Monitor* would be constructed in 100 days at his Brooklyn-based boatyard on the East River. She contained over 30 patented inventions, the most striking feature being her 200mm-thick plate armament, and single, steam-powered revolving cylindrical turret housing just two, but very powerful, 11-inch breech-loading main guns. Smaller than the CSS *Virginia* at 141 feet, and only crewed by 45 men once sea-worthy, she was immediately ordered to set sail for the U.S. Navy blockade at Hampton Roads where intelligence confirmed the Confederate ironclad was stationed.

The CSS *Virginia* steamed into open waters at noon on March 8, and with it, the face of naval warfare would irrevocably change. The squadron of five Union wooden-hulled warships with support vessels stationed to blockade Hampton Roads from the entrance to the open sea was at anchor, the largest being the sail-frigate the USS *Cumberland*. The *Virginia* made straight for her, enemy shells bouncing off her plate armor, until she finally ploughed into the Federal ship's hull with her ram, an act that almost sank both vessels. She broke free, and as the *Cumberland* sank, taking 150 of her crew with it, the Confederate ship now turned on *Cumberland's* sister ship, USS *Congress*. Attempting to avoid a similar fate, *Congress* had gone aground, the prone ship making an easy target for the *Virginia's* gunners. An offer of surrender was in motion when Union shore batteries fired upon the *Virginia* whose crew, in retaliation, sent hot shot into the *Congress*, burning the hull and causing her magazine to eventually explode, killing 110 of her crew. As dusk began to settle, the *Virginia* retired back to port to prepare for the next day.

At dawn the next day, the USS *Monitor* finally arrived, her crew seasick and tired from their 48-hour voyage from Brooklyn but itching to now test their ironclad in battle and protect what remained of the Union fleet. Purportedly watched by 10,000 spectators, the two ships spent the next four hours battering away at each other, with *Virginia*'s smokestack shot away, and *Monitor*'s breech-loading cannons proving difficult to fire. By the early afternoon, *Virginia*'s gunners concentrated their fire on *Monitor*'s pilothouse, a small iron blockhouse near her bow. A shell splinter blinded the *Monitor*'s commanding officer, Lt. John L. Worden, forcing another withdrawal until he could be relieved. By the time she was ready to return to the fight, *Virginia* had turned away toward Norfolk. It had been a bloody draw.

The Confederate Navy's "super weapon" to break the Union blockade had failed, and the threat posed by Union forces driving into *Virginia* resulted in the *Virginia*'s scuttling two months later.

RIGHT Lt. Cdr., U.S. Navy, in standard Navy officer's dress during the Civil War. (Ron Volstad © Osprey Publishing)

THE BATTLE OF GLORIETA PASS
March 26–28, 1862

The least-known theater of war in the Civil War was that in the far west, where both sides contested for dominance of the New Mexico Territory. The forces they could call upon were far fewer than the tens of thousands fighting in the east, but nevertheless it was strategically important. The South wished to enforce its claim to the Confederate Arizona Territory with hoped-for support from local secessionists it believed were willing to rise up. To this end, President Jefferson Davis was persuaded by Maj. Henry Hopkins Sibley to sponsor an ambitious plan to develop new supply routes out west.

Sibley, a Louisianan, was a hard-drinking veteran of the Mexican–American War who had resigned his commission in the U.S. Army. He travelled to Richmond to outline to Davis' government how a small, well-supplied force under his command could capture the American West for the Confederacy. His plan was to raise troops in Texas and then march them north through Utah and Nevada to reach the silver- and gold-mining fields in California. Claiming this precious resource would not only help fund the Confederate economy, he would also seize control of the Californian shipping ports that were free of any Union blockade, and also the Transcontinental Railroad bases. In the process, his invasion would provoke local secessionists to rise up and support his men with supplies and accommodation. Davis gave Sibley the rank of brigadier general and the necessary paperwork to raise an army—which he would title the Army of New Mexico.

LEFT When actual mounted cavalry battles took place, they were simply mounted brawls, with little command and control. (Gerry Embleton © Osprey Publishing)

In February 1862, with a force of 2,590 men now raised, Sibley took to the field in New Mexico with an aim to defeat local Union forces, capture the state capital Santa Fe, and march onto California. Ironically, his Union opponent was Col. Edward Canby, a former friend he had served with in peacetime. Although well matched in numbers, Canby's small command of Regular U.S. Army soldiers was bolstered by local volunteers. The first encounter at Valverde led to the rebels winning control of the field, but the Union troops remaining undefeated behind their strong defenses of Fort Craig—the largest fort in the state. Now deciding to move north through the Rio Grande Valley, Sibley captured Santa Fe and Albuquerque on March 10, but both places were empty of supplies. Equally, the lack of local support, forcing his men to forage for food and water, made Sibley decide to capture the Federal supply base at Fort Union, 40 miles to the southwest.

As Sibley's forces moved toward Fort Union, he dispatched a force of 300 mounted Texan volunteers commanded by Maj. Charles L. Pyron to Apache Canyon at one end of Glorieta Pass with which to guarantee his column access to the High Plains of the Santa Fe Trail. He was unaware, however, that at the same time a thousand-strong column of Union volunteers of the 1st Colorado Infantry led by Col. John Slough had reached Fort Union and were now heading straight toward the same position.

Slough split his command, ordering Maj. John M. Chivington to take five companies of infantry and cavalry to Apache Canyon. On March 26, Pyron's men skirmished with Chivington's force in a fight that would last for a few hours, the Union capturing several Confederates before they retired to a defensive position further down the canyon. Both sides gathered reinforcements the next day.

On March 28, the strengthened Confederates under Lt. Col. William Scurry quickly moved down the canyon to attack the Federal positions. Although putting up a fierce defense, Slough's men were slowly beaten back toward Pigeon's Ranch a few miles away. The fighting dragged on throughout the day, as superior Confederate numbers told in attacks on the

Federal left and right flanks, and by dusk Slough retreated eastward from the field of battle toward Kozlowski's Ranch. It was here that providence handed strategic victory to the Union.

Chivington's command, with gunfire from the fighting echoing across the valley, had failed to attack the Confederate rear but instead by sheer luck came across Sibley's unprotected supply train of 80 wagons and 500 horses and mules. Led by Lt. Col. Manuel Chaves, the Federals descended upon it, killing the few Confederate guards, capturing the livestock, and destroying the wagons and supplies. Without proper supplies to support the expedition, the rebels had to retreat and would ultimately fall back all the way to San Antonio, Texas.

Sibley's ambition to capture Fort Union and with it conquer the Southwest for the Confederacy lay in the ashes of his burning supply column. Glorieta Pass was the climax of the Confederate invasion of New Mexico.

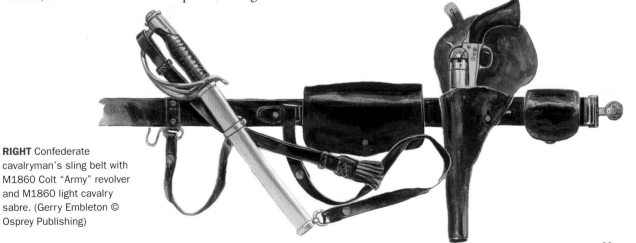

RIGHT Confederate cavalryman's sling belt with M1860 Colt "Army" revolver and M1860 light cavalry sabre. (Gerry Embleton © Osprey Publishing)

THE BATTLE OF SHILOH
April 6–7, 1862

In the western theater, if Union forces could win control of the Mississippi River, it would split the Confederacy in two and threaten its heartland of Georgia. With the capture of the key forts defending Mississippi, three Union armies comprising over 110,000 men now occupied key jumping-off points into the nearby states of Tennessee and Kentucky. The Confederacy's fears of a possible invasion into its very heartlands were made real. The Southern command had to take the initiative and repel the invaders.

Under the supervision of Gen. Albert Sidney Johnston, a new Army of the Mississippi of 40,000 men was created by bringing together formations from five different commands across the south, traveling via riverboats, trains, and forced marching, to coalesce at Corinth. Its aim would be to launch a surprise counteroffensive against Grant now camped 23 miles to the north at Pittsburg Landing on the Tennessee River, near Shiloh Church. For Johnston and President Jefferson Davis, timing was crucial in order that the intended target would not be reinforced by Maj. Gen. Don Carlos Buell's 50,000-strong army stationed outside of Nashville to the northeast. He knew that if Grant's army could be destroyed at Shiloh, the balance of power in the west might shift decisively in his favor.

On April 6 at 6am, Johnston's forces attacked, their goal to destroy Grant's left flank, drive a wedge between it and the artillery based on the Union gunboats by the Tennessee River, and give the demoralized enemy no option but to escape through the swamps of Snake and Owl Creeks and to their doom. The heavy rainfall of the previous two days would cause a fateful delay for

LEFT Gen. Braxton Bragg orders a fresh assault on the Union position the "Hornet's Nest," where the battle raged for several hours. (Alan Perry © Osprey Publishing)

41

Confederate troops to be in position for the battle. A lack of Union skirmishers and scouts forward of his positions fatally compromised Grant's ability to comprehend how significant this sudden assault along his 3-mile front actually was. Initial Confederate success was undone as formations became intermingled through the dense foliage, with their commanders confused as to intended targets. It would become the hallmark of the day's fighting as individual units and isolated commanders took control as best they could to win their respective encounters.

Thousands of Union stragglers now retreated toward the safety of Pittsburg Landing where Union gunboats continued to offer suppressing fire, while those units still fighting held precious ground to buy time for Grant to organize a new defensive line. Defeat seemed inevitable.

By mid-morning, the battle now raged at what became known as the "Hornet's Nest," a Union position set along a sunken farm road which acted as a barrier to the final Union position by the riverbank. Grant ordered his divisions to "maintain that position at all hazards." For several hours, a ferocious mini battle ensued as a full corps of Confederates launched a series of sporadic and uncoordinated attacks across an open field, which the Union defenders used to their advantage to bloody effect.

Amid the confusion and miscommunication between local commanders, Maj. Gen. Braxton Bragg failed to concentrate his overwhelming superiority against the Union line, whose cannister and artillery fire kept the Confederate frontal assaults at bay with murderous precision. Bragg finally assembled a 50-gun artillery park to blast the "Hornet's Nest" into submission. Johnston took it upon himself to personally lead the final assault and reeled in his saddle from a Union bullet striking behind his right knee. What seemed a superficial wound quickly escalated to a fatal one as he unwittingly bled to death for the lack of on-the-ground medical care. The "Hornet's Nest" finally capitulated—2,200 out of 11,000 were left to be taken prisoner. They had bought Grant time to rescue the battle as he set up a final defensive line and awaited reinforcements from Buell. It had been the bloodiest day's fighting in American history thus far.

Johnston's second-in-command, Gen. P.G.T. Beauregard, now took charge of what he believed to be a victorious battlefield, unaware that Grant was welcoming whole divisions of fresh troops to his lines. At 5:30am Grant hit the startled Confederates bedded down in captured Union lines, driving them back, and by mid-afternoon had retaken the field with the Army of the Mississippi contemplating an ordered retreat back toward Corinth, having lost 10,000 men dead or wounded. The exhausted Union troops did not engage further; the battle was over. The slaughter had been unimaginable, equal to that of the Battle of Waterloo, and was openly reported in the Northern press, bringing home to the public just what a bloody attritional war it was going to be.

ABOVE The 12-pdr Napoleonic gun attached to the limber. (Tony Bryan © Osprey Publishing)

THE BATTLE OF GAINES' MILL— THE SEVEN DAYS

June 27, 1862

By the summer of the second year of the Civil War, the fortunes of the Confederacy were plummeting. The early Southern euphoria at the victory at First Bull Run had not been followed by other victories. Instead, the next 11 months had brought many defeats, both in the eastern and western theaters, and now, with the Army of the Potomac led by Maj. Gen. George McClellan camped on the Tidewater Peninsula and heading toward Richmond, Union forces were only a few miles from the Southern capital.

President Jefferson Davis had found the right man for the job of defending Richmond—Gen. Robert E. Lee. McClellan would misjudge Lee's ability as a fighting general, and from June 26, for the next seven days Lee would constantly attack the lumbering Union army, seizing the initiative. The fight at Gaines' Mill would prove to be the key battle that succeeded in pushing the Army of the Potomac away from Richmond and have McClellan lose his nerve and retreat in the face of a weaker enemy.

Lee, at first, had ordered Richmond to be encircled with formidable entrenchments, earning him the nickname "King of Spades," but he had no intention of sitting behind them and waiting to be attacked. His strategy was to leave a small proportion of the newly titled Army of Northern Virginia to guard the capital while he took the rest of it to circumnavigate the bulk of Union positions and fall heavily on their flank at the

LEFT The charge of the 4th Texas at Gaines' Mill. (Stephen Walsh © Osprey Publishing)

northern end of the Chickahominy River. Reinforced with the 20,000 men of the Army of the Shenandoah, commanded by Maj. Gen. "Stonewall" Jackson—a title earned for his stubborn defence at First Manassas—Lee had a formidable force of over 100,000 troops and was armed with the detailed positioning of McClellan's lines provided by the mounted reconnaissance of Maj. Gen. J.E.B. Stuart.

The first day's battle saw Confederate troops hitting the isolated V Corps guarding the Union northern flank and the road toward the Federal supply base at Mechanicsville, commanded by Brig. Gen. Fitz John Porter. Lee's army was to pin him down, while Jackson's army would turn his flank and start the collapse of the whole Union line. However, Jackson was not in position due to delays, and Lee's frontal attack against Porter's positions along Beaver Dam Creek, a

boggy stream that fed into the Chickahominy, went in piecemeal. Well-sited Union artillery and solid discipline enabled V Corps to fight them off, and by day's end Confederate casualties were high. Despite this setback, an unnerved McClellan believed he now not only faced superior numbers to his front outside of Richmond, but on his northern flank, too. Despite urgings from his subordinates to attack the weakened capital, he refused, losing his chance to take the city and thus isolate Lee in the north from any reinforcements. With Stonewall Jackson's units now in position and threatening to cut V Corps off from the rest of the Union army behind the river, McClellan ordered Porter to pull back to new entrenched positions at Gaines' Mill, closer to the

Chickahominy, protecting the main crossing of it and the road that led to his main supply depot of White House Landing. If Lee could crush V Corps now, McClellan would be cut off from his main base of supply and forced to retreat.

Counting on McClellan's timidity, Lee now seized his opportunity, launching what would be the largest Confederate infantry attack of the whole war against V Corps. Six divisions totaling 57,000 men advanced in echelon over difficult ground that made progress under sustained Union fire from their entrenchments murderous. Although a difficult position to assault, Lee's commanders again failed to follow his plans, with their units uncoordinated and heavily beaten back as a result.

With heavy casualties from the day's failed assaults, Lee took a last throw of the dice to break the Federal line, sending in Hood's division, their "rebel yell" echoing around the battlefield as they came on. It would be the 4th Texas who broke through the first line of defense, forcing the Union troops to pull back in chaos as the rebels charged up to the crest, overrunning Porter's artillery. V Corps withdrew under rebel fire across the Chickahominy, burning the bridges behind them. They had suffered over 30 percent casualties—6,837 men—while Lee's losses were higher—a total of 7,993 men. Gaines' Mill was the bloodiest day of the war thus far in the eastern theater and would prove to be the fatal point for McClellan's army as he began a retreat from Richmond and off the peninsula.

ABOVE Standard of the 2nd US Cavalry Regiment. Redesignated the 5th in 1861, it fought at Gaines' Mill. (Rick Scollins © Osprey Publishing)

LEFT Maj. Gen. George McClellan led the Army of the Potomac at the Battle of Gaines' Mill. (Richard Hook © Osprey Publishing)

THE BATTLE OF SECOND MANASSAS/ SECOND BULL RUN

August 29–30, 1862

By the summer of 1862, President Lincoln had decided the eastern theater needed a new man to run it. The disaster at First Bull Run under Brig. Gen. Irvin McDowell had led to his demotion to take charge of a single corps. His replacement, Maj. Gen. George McClellan, had been outfoxed by Robert E. Lee during the Seven Days battles outside of the Confederate capital Richmond, resulting in the Army of the Potomac becoming marooned on the peninsula in their entrenchments. Relieving McClellan of his dual commands, Lincoln now installed Henry Halleck as general-in-chief, and Maj. Gen. John Pope to lead

Union troops in the eastern theater with a new formation—the Army of Virginia—to be reinforced with McClellan's men. Like his president, Pope hailed from Kentucky but had relocated to Illinois, and in the early days of the war had enjoyed some localized success in the western theater.

Pope's bombastic claims of what a successful commander from the western theater might accomplish were mocked by his own officers and men, while his Southern opponents loathed his thirst to prosecute a "total war" in Virginia. It was said that Lee could not wait to test this "miscreant" in the field. He would soon have his chance, as Pope sought to fulfill the two objectives set for him: ensure the defense of Washington by thwarting any Confederate thrust from the Shenandoah Valley, and

LEFT Low on ammunition, the men of the Louisiana Brigade resort to hurling stones at the onrushing Federals. (Mike Adams © Osprey Publishing)

attempt to draw Lee away from Richmond to face destruction.

The might of two Federal armies was now under Pope's command, forcing Lee to go on the offensive to tackle them separately before they could combine and overwhelm Richmond. He divided his army, leaving a token force to tie down McClellan and the Army of the Potomac, while heavy reinforcements traveled north to Maj. Gen. Thomas "Stonewall" Jackson's Army of the Shenandoah in order to thwart Union plans. The Confederates seized Gordonsville, a key railroad supply hub, forcing Pope to retreat northwards 30 miles toward Culpepper Court House and wait for his whole army to assemble. Jackson continued his advance, winning a costly victory at Cedar Mountain on August 9, and then waited for Lee and his trusted subordinate Maj. Gen. James Longstreet (commanding the army's right wing) to join him by the Rapidan River. Against all military logic, Lee divided his army again, this time sending Jackson on August 25 to skirt around the Union flank by forced march through Thoroughfare Gap, reaching the Union supply depot at Manassas Junction and threatening Union lines of communications.

Despite Confederate cavalry screening Jackson's movements, Pope now finally realized he faced Jackson's whole corps and drew up plans to isolate and destroy him, unaware of Longstreet's and Lee's forces nearby. On the morning of August 29, Jackson's brigades took up positions on an old railway embankment west of Manassas Junction. As four separate Union assaults assailed them— the final one only being held back by his men hurling rocks at the Federals once their ammunition had run out—Jackson still held his position. By evening, both sides had settled for a decisive end the following day, Pope in the mistaken belief he now had the Confederates on the run at last, while Jackson was now joined by Lee and Longstreet for the final battle.

Pope ordered a "general pursuit" of the rebels the next morning. They ran into trouble almost immediately. Longstreet's artillery decimated the Union attacks, and by late afternoon Lee ordered a "general advance" to drive Pope from the field. Jackson's and Longstreet's wings collapsed both Union flanks as they retreated back to the banks of Bull Run. Although managing to successfully withdraw and realign the next day, by September 1, with another march by Jackson's "Foot Cavalry" threatening his right flank, Pope ordered a Federal retreat back to the safety of Washington's fortifications.

The fighting had been far more brutal than that at First Bull Run, with over 22,000 casualties. The South was jubilant that Pope had been driven out of eastern Virginia, marking the end of his tenure as the head of Union forces in the eastern theater. He would be transferred to the west to fight the Sioux. For Lee, Longstreet, Jackson, and the Army of Northern Virginia, they had proven once and for all that it was a power to be reckoned with. The way was now open for a strike northward into Maryland and to take the war to the Union.

ABOVE The flag of 2nd Division, V Corps, which fought at Second Bull Run under Brig. Gen. George Sykes. (Rick Scollins © Osprey Publishing)

RIGHT A rear view of the soft knapsack carried by Union infantrymen during the Civil War. (John White © Osprey Publishing)

THE BATTLE OF ANTIETAM/ SHARPSBURG

September 17, 1862

The Confederacy's first invasion of the North would begin with Lee's army of 55,000 men moving into Maryland, aware that a further victory over the Army of the Potomac might precipitate foreign intervention from Britain and France to force a negotiated peace.

After the setback at Second Bull Run under Maj. Gen. Polk, President Lincoln now replaced him with their previous commander, Maj. Gen. George B. McClellan. McClellan was a superb administrator but lacked the killer instinct. But as both sides tracked one another through Maryland, McClellan was provided with the discovery of the Confederate's battle plan—Special Order 191—detailing their movements in the surrounding countryside.

McClellan now knew Lee's army was split into three columns and could be picked off and destroyed piecemeal. Yet he did not act but sat on the information for a crucial 18 hours, allowing Lee time to coalesce the greater portion of his forces and set about building defensive works along Antietam Creek and await attack from forces coming to destroy him. His men were protected by woods, sunken roads, and Antietam Creek, which could be crossed by three bridges, but his position was still precarious if attacked along a broad front simultaneously.

It would be a battle of three phases. At dawn, on Lee's left flank, Maj. Gen. Joseph Hooker's I Corps advanced up the Hagerstown Pike to dislodge the

LEFT The 6th Wisconsin of the Iron Brigade charge through the cornfield, the site of some of the bloodiest fighting at Antietam. (John White © Osprey Publishing)

7,000 men of "Stonewall" Jackson from a plateau on which sat a whitewashed church belonging to a local sect of German Baptists. The fighting here would be fierce, as both sides fought for possession of cornfields that would change hands 15 times. Whole regiments entered the fray and disappeared in a firestorm of cannon and musketry. By 10am, two Union commanders had left the field wounded, and combined casualties stood at 13,000 men.

The battle now opened upon the center of the Confederate line as Maj. Gen. Edwin V. Sumner's Union II Corps moved toward the sunken road occupied by Maj. Gen. D.H. Hill's division of 2,500 men. Although heavily outnumbered, the Confederates had strong natural defensive works to beat back the brigade-strength waves of blue. As the carnage continued, both sides reinforced until all of Lee's reserves had been used, and, significantly, many of his subordinate commanders overseeing the defense were out of action.

Union infantry finally exposed a weak point in the line and began enfilading fire into the startled Southerners, wreaking havoc. In three hours, across an area of several hundred yards, over 5,000 men would fall, thus christening the position "Bloody Lane." The situation was further exacerbated when a miscommunication had what remained of the Confederate center about-face with the intent to retreat back to Sharpsburg. Maj. Gen. James Longstreet's quick actions with a counterattack and artillery fire drove the Federals back to their original starting points, but still McClellan didn't respond with reinforcements to exploit the position.

By the afternoon, the focus of Union attacks now shifted to the southern end of the Confederate line where Lee's weakened right flank—he had taken various units away from this sector to reinforce along his northern lines—awaited to repulse Maj. Gen. Ambrose Burnside's 12,000-strong X Corps, which advanced against 3,000 Confederates holding the ridges heading toward Sharpsburg. A small force of 400 Georgians defended the vital stone-bridge crossing. Burnside sent in his forces one brigade at a time through this bottleneck, which were repulsed by the Georgians time and again, until finally the 51st Pennsylvania established a bridgehead and a push on to Sharpsburg was expected imminently.

In the nick of time, as Burnside took another two hours to bring up supplies of ammunition, the light division of A.P. Hill arrived after a 17-mile forced march from Harpers Ferry. They slammed into the advancing Federals, who by now were a mere 200 yards from capturing Sharpsburg itself, driving them back toward the creek and to the bridge they had expended so much blood capturing. An unnerved Burnside, not realizing he still outnumbered this new force, begged McClellan for reinforcements, but despite two corps in reserve, he refused. By 5:30pm, all was quiet along the line as both sides recovered from the carnage they had inflicted upon one another.

The next day, both sides recovered their dead and exchanged their wounded under a flag of truce. Lee's battered army retreated toward the safety of Virginia, having suffered 31 percent casualties. Though a pyrrhic victory, Lincoln now seized the moment to announce his Emancipation Proclamation for the South's 3.5 million slaves, which secured the goal of discouraging foreign intervention for a negotiated settlement.

RIGHT Flag of the 21st Mississippi Infantry Regiment, a Confederate unit which fought at the Battle of Antietam. (Rick Scollins © Osprey Publishing)

THE BATTLE OF FREDERICKSBURG
December 13, 1862

By early November 1862, an impatient President Lincoln had installed Maj. Gen. Ambrose Burnside as the new commander of the Army of the Potomac. Burnside's ambitious plan to defeat Lee began with a rapid advance to Fredericksburg situated on the Rappahannock River, where they would seize the town and then march on to the Confederate capital at Richmond in order to overwhelm the city—thus taking the strategic initiative and forcing the Army of Northern Virginia to fight on ground of the Union's choosing.

Lincoln readily endorsed the plan, unaware of the unhealthy state of the Army of the Potomac, which was now over 140,000 strong and reorganized into three Grand Divisions, each comprising two corps, whose commanders loathed, or at best resented, their new leader. Equally difficult for Burnside was the poor state of the communication and supply chains between him and the War Department back in Washington, which would prove both calamitous for his plans and deadly for his troops.

Burnside's strategy began to unravel almost as soon as the Army of the Potomac moved to the crossing points from their base at Falmouth on November 17, where the Right Grand Division, commanded by Maj. Gen. Edwin V. Sumner, found themselves with no pontoons to ford the fast-flowing river. Union engineers had reported they had not the horse trains to transport the pontoon bridges overland. Sumner was anxious to get across to the town and take the heights beyond, which were lightly defended; however, fearful that they might be stranded across a flooded

LEFT The charge of Irish Brigade on Marye's Heights, a key Confederate position in the Battle of Fredericksburg. (Adam Hook © Osprey Publishing)

barrier, Burnside ordered a halt and demanded his boats and pontoons be made ready as soon as possible. A few days dragged into weeks, and by the end of the month the element of surprise had evaporated, and Lee had moved his two corps of 79,000 men to defensive works in the hills behind Fredericksburg, ready and well positioned to await an expected Union assault.

The Confederates established formidable lines of defense stretching for many miles north and south of Fredericksburg, including the key position of Marye's Heights situated 600 yards to the west of the town, and commanded by Maj. Gen. Longstreet's corps. Robert E. Lee's troops and artillery had an excellent field of fire should the enemy get across a canal and into the main field to then attack

the position. His commanders had excellent internal lines of supply and communication, making it possible for any breaks in their defenses to be reinforced. Even if the Federals did intend carrying the ridge, they would first need to take positions protected by a 4-foot-high stone wall a few hundred yards in front, where four lines of infantry of Brig. Gen. Thomas R. Cobb's Georgian Division would pour fire down upon them.

On December 12, after a heavy artillery bombardment that wrecked the town, crossing pontoon bridges erected under intense fire, Union troops established a bridgehead and slowly pushed back the Confederates through its streets, until by 4:30pm all had been cleared for the massed columns to start crossing for the main attack the next day.

The Army of the Potomac attacked on the morning of December 13 as the freezing fog was lifting off the Rappahannock. On the south flank of Fredericksburg, stretching out several hundred yards, some progress was made by Federal advances of Maj. Gen. William B. Franklin's Left Grand Division, only to be thwarted by strong rebel counterattacks and poor coordination of Union reinforcements, which led to heavy casualties.

The main thrust now came at Marye's Heights, where Sumner was ordered to send "a division or more" to seize the high ground and thus to then allow him to roll up Lee's right flank. At noon, the first of several divisions, a brigade at a time, went in, each to face intense artillery fire as they double-timed in rank up to the Confederate positions, and each division melted before the firestorm meted out by Lt. Gen. Longstreet's corps behind the stone wall. The most gallant charge of the day was made by the Irish Brigade led by Gen. Thomas Meagher, green sprigs of boxwood in their kepis. They got to within 25 paces of the stone wall before they were driven back by a tempest of rebel fire from the 24th Georgia (also an Irish formation), who cheered their countrymen's heroism as they fell back. By the evening, as the light started to fade and 14 attacks had been repulsed, the route up to Marye's Heights was littered with the dead and dying—almost 9,000 men.

A distraught Burnside resolved to lead the next day's attacks personally in atonement for the disaster but was talked down by his subordinates. Instead, he ordered a withdrawal back across the Rappahannock. Lee's casualties of 5,377 were light compared with the Union figure of 12,653, over which the Southern press crowed as their Northern cousins fumed. Burnside was relieved of command as Lincoln continued to look for a Union general who could deliver him victory.

THE BATTLE OF CHANCELLORSVILLE
April 30–May 6, 1863

Despite the enormous casualties suffered at Fredericksburg the previous winter, the new commander of the Army of the Potomac, Maj. Gen. "Fighting Joe" Hooker, still commanded a formidable force of 130,000 men now encamped at Falmouth, Virginia. By April, he had successfully reorganized the unwieldy Grand Division structure to a more sensible corps formation, with an independent cavalry wing. Just as significantly, he improved his men's morale, having them adopt specific insignia for their units, improving supplies, implementing more drilling, and giving the Army of the Potomac back its esprit de corps.

He realized that to bring Lee to battle on ground of his choosing he must first threaten the Confederate

capital, Richmond. On April 27, 10,000 Union horse crossed the Rappahannock upstream, to then swing around Lee's rear and attack his supply lines. At the same time, another corps crossed downstream, while three more corps of infantry crossed the Rappahannock and Rapidan rivers and marched as planned toward the hamlet of Chancellorsville to the west—the area so named after the large brick mansion, which dominated the major crossroads cutting through the dense woods. By May 1, Hooker had over 70,000 troops situated around Chancellorsville awaiting what he was sure would either be a doomed Confederate frontal assault, or their withdrawal.

Lee had been taken by surprise, but realizing the troops at Chancellorsville were the immediate threat, he gambled and divided his smaller force to attack a portion of the Union army before it had time to gather itself. He left 11,000 men above Fredericksburg to

LEFT Gen. Lee on horseback at the front of his advancing troops at Chancellorsville. (Adam Hook © Osprey Publishing)

hold in place Union forces, and with Maj. Gen. "Stonewall" Jackson's corps marched to Chancellorsville with 40,000 troops.

The three-day battle began mid-morning on May 1, as Hooker's columns advanced to capture a strategic crossroads, unaware that Stonewall Jackson's forces were there, too. The fighting had been fairly even, yet Hooker became anxious. The realization that his enemy had not retreated from such superior forces and instead wished to fight had spoiled his strategy and shaken his confidence. Against the wishes of his corps commanders, he ordered Union troops back behind their original fortifications, not only giving up valuable high ground, but handing the initiative back to Lee.

The Union army was now stretched out for several miles, anchored on the left flank by the Rappahannock River to the east, with strong fortifications in the center; right on the farthest point, surrounded by thick woods, was XI Corps led by Maj. Gen. Oliver Howard. Such was Howard's belief in his natural defenses that he had shied away from Hooker's general order for all corps commanders to construct fortifications; it would prove his downfall.

That night, Lee and Jackson sat in conference debating an audacious idea. Lee would again divide his forces in the face of superior numbers and have Jackson take his 2nd Corps of 28,000 men through the back roads of the Wilderness—a wide area of dense shrubs

and trees— to position himself at the flank of XI Corps, while Lee held at bay the bulk of Hooker's army facing him. Using a local guide, Jackson's men set out at 4am, reaching their destination by 5pm after a 12-mile march.

Jackson's men hit XI Corps like a sledgehammer, enveloping the startled Union troops as Hooker's whole line retreated before his eyes. Darkness saved a total Union collapse, as both sides halted and dug in where they stood. Jackson and his staff ventured ahead of the Confederate line to assess if a night-time attack could work. As they returned, rebel pickets mistook them for Union cavalry and opened fire, killing two and wounding Jackson himself, his corps led by Maj. Gen. J.E.B. Stuart.

Lee and Stuart now needed to eliminate III Corps, which stood between them, if they were to bring both halves of the Confederate Army together to then drive the remaining Federals from the battlefield. Hooker gave up an elevated position at Hazel Grove, allowing the Confederates to take it and establish a formidable gun park which would dominate the rest of the day's fighting. A fierce morning of assaults by Stuart's men began on May 3, as they crashed into the center of the Union positions. Unable to command and realizing if any one Union unit now broke, then his whole army was in peril, Hooker ordered a withdrawal. It was a crushing defeat.

It would later be described as the "perfect battle," but the cost to the South was enormous in terms of casualties they could ill afford and the fatal wounding of their legendary general Stonewall Jackson.

LEFT The Headquarters flag, I Corps. The unit fought at Chancellorsville under the command of Maj. Gen. John F. Reynolds. (Rick Scollins © Osprey Publishing)

THE SIEGE OF VICKSBURG

May 18–July 4, 1863

The cotton-trading fortress of Vicksburg was known as the "Gibraltar of the Confederacy" due to its key strategic position on the Mississippi River; it was the largest city in the state. At the outbreak of the war, the U.S. War Department had been skeptical of any strategy that involved taking control of the Mississippi and Tennessee rivers, which in effect would split the Confederate states in two and guarantee the Union forces dominance of their supply lines. Only multiple defeats in the eastern theater against Robert E. Lee's Army of Northern Virginia forced Washington to see that taking the Mississippi and organizing a naval blockade of the Confederate coastline could mean ultimate victory. Now, President Lincoln himself knew that the key to this working was to overcome the main obstacle—Vicksburg.

LEFT The USS *Mound City* running past Vicksburg, April 1863. (Tony Bryan © Osprey Publishing)

Vicksburg held a commanding position above the Mississippi River, where the currents were extremely strong as it flowed the final few hundred miles out to the Gulf of Mexico. The nature of its surrounding terrain of back swamps, small lakes, and boggy land surrounded by dense trees and shrubs gave the impression it was impregnable to any attacking force. This was the obstacle facing the Union commander tasked with taking it, Maj. Gen. Ulysses S. Grant, fresh from his bloody victory at Shiloh, leading the Army of the Tennessee of approximately 75,000 men. He was at the height of his powers as a fighting general and fortunate to have many able subordinates, such as Maj. Gen. Tecumseh Sherman, and his adjutant general, John A. Rawlins. The job of defending the city and commanding its garrison of 38,000 troops fell to Lt. Gen. John C. Pemberton, a Northerner, and more of an administrator than a leader of men.

Union attempts to take Vicksburg before Grant arrived to take charge in March 1863 had all failed from either a lack of troops or not enough naval gunboats to dominate the fortress. By the time Grant arrived, it had been heavily reinforced, and all attempts made by the Army of the Tennessee to take the city failed, leading to a stalemate and for Grant to become morose, bored, and keen to drink. The Northern media recounted many stories of his drinking bouts while at his headquarters—a situation that needed a dramatic solution.

Grant now decided he would take the bulk of his command, march them down the western side of the Mississippi in order to cross the river below Vicksburg, and then tackle all that the swamps of the Mississippi Delta could throw at them to come up behind the rear of the city, cut off its supply lines, and lay siege to it. It was a bold move; for three weeks Grant's men were out of communication in enemy territory, with limited supplies as they marched on improvised roads for 180 miles, winning five pitched battles as the Confederates tried to thwart their progress. By May 18, Union troops surrounded Vicksburg and began to construct siegeworks facing the city, as well as entrenchments facing outwards to protect their rear from further attacks.

Over the next few days, Grant ordered direct assaults on the city's defenses. All were repulsed, with over 3,000 casualties, but the writing was now on the wall for the rebels, as they considered evacuating the garrison. All attempts by local Confederate forces close to Vicksburg now failed in cutting Grant's supply lines or driving off the naval blockade.

Every day, over 200 guns were pounding the city, as its inhabitants cowered in the caves they dug into the yellow clay of the bluffs by the river. Food supplies dwindled until all the horses, mules, dogs, and rats had been eaten by the Vicksburg citizens who were mocked by their besiegers as living in "Prairie Dog Town." The garrison itself was on a daily ration of a handful of peas and rice with one cup of water—in the height of summer. After 48 days of nonstop bombardment, Pemberton finally gave in, not wishing to put his men and the civilian population through any further "cruel inhumanity."

It was a startling victory for the Union, and on the national holiday of the Fourth of July the Stars and Stripes at last flew above the capitol building in Vicksburg. It came as the second major blow to the Confederacy, as in the east, Lee's defeat at Gettysburg the previous day saw him retreat from Pennsylvania. For Grant, it was now the second time he had taken the surrender of a Confederate army. This, however, was a far bigger victory, as the gateway of the Mississippi had been opened to the Union, as President Lincoln exclaimed: "The Father of Waters flows again!"

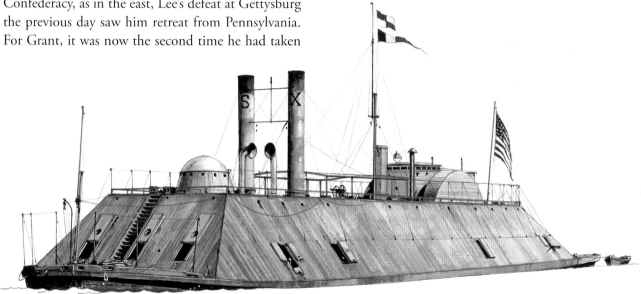

ABOVE The USS *Essex*, which saw service at Vicksburg. (Tony Bryan © Osprey Publishing)

THE BATTLE OF BRANDY STATION
June 9, 1863

Fought as Robert E. Lee's Army of Northern Virginia began its second invasion of the North, which would culminate at Gettysburg on July 1–3, the Battle of Brandy Station in Virginia was the largest cavalry engagement on American soil and would ultimately demonstrate that the much-derided Union cavalryman was now the equal of his vaunted Southern opponent.

Fresh from its stunning victory at Chancellorsville a few weeks before, the Confederate army comprising 72,000 men was leaving its encampments around Culpepper County and heading into Pennsylvania as part of the grand plan of bringing the Union government to the negotiating table through force. Lee was also eager to replenish his weakened forces with

LEFT The now experienced Union cavalrymen proved their worth at the Battle of Brandy Station in Virginia. (Adam Hook © Osprey Publishing)

much-needed supplies that he knew the rich farmsteads of the Northern states would contain. As they awaited orders to march, the army sat in camp, protected by the screen of 9,500 cavalrymen held within five brigades and commanded by the flamboyant Maj. Gen. J.E.B. Stuart. Thus far in the war, the Southern horsemen had bested their Northern enemy on countless occasions, through their dash, horsemanship, tactics, and leadership. They were the shock troops of the South, with a reputation to match.

Unbeknownst to Stuart, however, 11,000 Federal troops, mainly mounted and supported with some infantry units, led by Maj. Gen. Alfred Pleasonton, were about to spoil the party. Under orders from the Army of the Potomac's commander, Maj. Gen. Joseph Hooker, still smarting from his reverse at Chancellorsville in May, the Union cavalry was to "disperse and destroy" the rebel forces through a surprise pincer attack across the Rappahannock River as the dawn fog shielded their movements. Although they would catch Stuart's mounted forces napping as they crossed at two points—Beverly's Ford and Kelley's Ford—Pleasonton would himself be surprised at the size of the force he attacked.

At 4:30am, the brigade of the veteran Kentuckian cavalry commander John Buford crossed the Rappahannock, easily pushing back the Confederate skirmishers until he was established at the bend of Beverly's Ford, threatening Stuart's artillery park. The Southern cavalry brigade of William E. Jones saved the situation by storming into Buford's leading units, some of his men riding half-naked and bareback into action, holding the Federals back while the Confederate guns were limbered up and repositioned as the overall battle began to unfold. The brigades of Jones and Wade Hampton now formed either side of the guns, establishing a formidable obstacle to any further Northern advance toward the main encampment at Brandy Station. Despite this, the charge of the 6th Pennsylvania Cavalry was described as "brilliant and glorious" by onlookers as Buford attempted to maintain the momentum of the surprise attack. Though spectacular, the regiment would be beaten back and suffer the greatest casualties of any unit during the battle.

Buford attempted to outflank this line, but his men encountered a new line formed behind a stone wall and led by Robert E. Lee's son, Brig. Gen. "Rooney" Lee. Beating back sustained and costly attacks, Rooney Lee's force suddenly vacated the ground to Buford, as they realized a new mounted division led by Brig. Gen David Gregg (who, having been lost prior to the opening of hostilities, had now succeeded in crossing further along the river) was threatening Stuart at Brandy Station itself. These two columns that had crossed at Kelley's Ford made their way to their targets: one to the rail hub at Brandy Station, and the other to Stevensburg.

Although his rear at Brandy Station was under serious threat of becoming overrun, due to the timidity of the Union advance J.E.B. Stuart managed to reorganize his units, form new lines, and at first hold and then hit the

Union horsemen and infantry support along the low rise of Fleetwood Hill. The initial delay by the Union troops cost them dearly. The overall plan was compromised, as the battle developed into a series of charges and counter-charges. Pleasonton called an end to the operation, his forces re-crossing the Rappahannock after 14 hours of battle. Over 18,000 horsemen had fought one another to a standstill, with the Federals losing 907 men, while the Confederates suffered 523 casualties. Although technically winning, Stuart was heavily criticized for being caught off guard, for which he would try to atone with the army's advance into Pennsylvania, and which would have disastrous consequences for Lee's fate at Gettysburg a few weeks later.

RIGHT The Battle of Brandy Station was the largest predominantly cavalry engagement of the Civil War.
(Peter Dennis © Osprey Publishing)

THE BATTLE OF GETTYSBURG
July 1–3, 1863

Fought in and around the hills of the sleepy Pennsylvanian town, across three pivotal days in the high summer, Gettysburg is arguably the key battle of the entire Civil War. Robert E. Lee's invading Army of Northern Virginia, fresh from its dramatic victory at Chancellorsville, attempted to finally break the Union Army of the Potomac on its own territory and thus force a diplomatic solution to the war.

The Army of Northern Virginia had been hastily reorganized after the death of Lee's brilliant commander Thomas "Stonewall" Jackson. It now comprised three corps under the respective commands of Lt. Gens. James Longstreet (First), Richard S. Ewell (Second), and A.P. Hill (Third), totaling 72,000 men when strengthened by the four cavalry divisions of J.E.B. Stuart. Lee was confident of this second invasion of the North.

Now commanded by Maj. Gen. George Meade, the Army of the Potomac shadowed the Confederates through the Shenandoah Valley and into the North, not knowing where their actual target was but under instructions from Washington to ensure they did not threaten the city and, where possible, to be defeated.

Lee's plans were to head toward Harrisburg in northern Pennsylvania and then perhaps swing toward Washington itself and set his army between the capital and the pursuing Union forces who would be forced to fight an offensive action against Lee's defensive entrenchments—much as they had at Fredericksburg. However, the Army of Northern Virginia was marching blind due to their cavalry, led by Maj. Gen. J.E.B. Stuart, venturing too far away from the main body.

LEFT "Pickett's Charge," the infantry assault ordered by Gen. Robert E. Lee on the last day of the battle. (Adam Hook © Osprey Publishing)

Lee was unaware of how close the Federal army of 100,000 men actually was to his route of march, and at Gettysburg on July 1 they finally collided.

The first day of battle had a Confederate brigade under Brig. Gen. Henry Heth coming in from the north in search of supplies and a warehouse of shoes Confederate scouts had been told were situated in the town. They were unaware that Union cavalry of Brig. Gen. John Buford had ridden in from the south, spotted the Southerners, and realizing the town's strategic importance as a major crossroads, taken up defensive positions on the outskirts with the hope that reinforcements from I Corps would soon arrive. Meade's corps were travelling north independently of one another, but in close proximity in case of attack. As what was a skirmish

escalated into a major confrontation on that first critical day, the Confederate divisions overwhelmed the outnumbered Federals, driving them back through the town and into the surrounding hills to the south where they quickly established a defensive perimeter. Lee had now arrived to take command and issued orders for his troops to take the right flank of the Union line on Culp's Hill and leading to Cemetery Ridge; both attacks failed. Meade had also joined his commanders on the ground and agreed with their decision that their defensive position dictated they should stand and fight. More troops on both sides poured in as fighting died down for the day. Over 15,000 men had been killed, wounded or captured.

By the beginning of the second day of the battle, the Union lines now resembled a fishhook above the town, with Lee determined to drive them off with all-out assaults on both flanks, made famous by their names: Culp's Hill and Cemetery Hill on the Union right; the Wheatfield, Devil's Den, the Peach Orchard, and Little Round Top on the Union left. Both attacks in the afternoon were beaten off, with losses estimated at 20,000 killed, wounded or captured.

On the final day of battle, despite Longstreet's objections, Lee was still confident that diversionary attacks on the flanks would enable an all-out assault on the Federal center to succeed. He was convinced his men would succeed against the odds just as they had at Second Bull Run, Fredericksburg, and Chancellorsville. At 3pm, following a 150-gun artillery barrage, Maj. Gen. George Pickett led 12,500 Confederates, including his Virginia division, across a mile of open ground and into the teeth of a murderous field of Union fire. It ended in complete disaster with over half his command killed, wounded or captured.

A crestfallen Lee now had to lead his battered army through a torrential downpour back to the safety of northern Virginia as Meade's exhausted troops remained in their positions, much to President Lincoln's dismay, who believed the war could have been ended quickly. Over 50,000 troops fell at Gettysburg—the bloodiest casualty list of the entire war—and the cause of the Confederacy was fatally wounded.

LEFT Gen. Lee, commander of the Army of Northern Virginia at Gettysburg. (Adam Hook © Osprey Publishing)

ABOVE Flag of the Confederate 9th Virginia Infantry Regiment, which fought at Gettysburg. (Rick Scollins © Osprey Publishing)

THE SECOND BATTLE OF FORT WAGNER

July 18, 1863

Fort (or "Battery") Wagner would become synonymous with the bravery and sacrifice of the Union's first regiment raised from the African American community in the North—the 54th Massachusetts. Once President Abraham Lincoln's Emancipation Proclamation had come into effect at the beginning of 1863, Secretary of State for War Edwin M. Stanton had instructed the governor of Massachusetts, John A. Andrew, to begin raising all-black regiments from the free black communities in the North. In February, after several failed attempts, Governor Andrew persuaded Captain Robert Gould Shaw, from a prominent abolitionist

LEFT Starting out 650 strong, the assault on Fort Wagner cost the 54th almost half their men. (Peter Dennis © Osprey Publishing)

family in Long Island, New York, to become the new regimental commander. Promoted to colonel, Gould Shaw would now recruit fellow abolitionist white officers to staff the unit; by May it was mustered into service and marched out of Boston, heading for the Carolinas, where it became part of X Corps.

Charleston was a prominent and politically important city and harbor for the South's government. Secession had begun there in April 1861, and to many Southerners it was the cradle of their cause. By the summer of 1863, Union forces had been blockading the harbor and outlying area for many months, thus making it irrelevant as a supply base to Confederate forces. Nevertheless, to the Union, if they took the city, then the damage to Southern morale would be immense. Guarding the southern entrance to the harbor was a strip of land known as Morris Island, and at its tip was Fort (Battery) Wagner—a significant obstacle, with 30-foot-high walls and a 300-by-600-foot trench system. With a garrison of 1,600 troops protected in a bomb-proof bunker, ten heavy cannons stationed on the ramparts, and an effective mortar that could endanger Union ships out to sea, it was a tough nut to crack.

The Union X Corps, led by Brig. Gen. Quincy Gilmore, had attempted an earlier assault on July 11 and been bloodily repulsed, with 389 casualties. Before the second attack would go in a week later, Gilmore aimed to draw away Confederate reinforcements from the intended target by a secondary attack on the other side of the island at Grimball's Landing, combined with a major barrage against Fort Wagner itself. The only approach to the fort by infantry was filing through a

160-foot-wide strip of sandy beach that was sandwiched between the Atlantic Ocean to the east and a thick swamp to the west. The Union assault would consist of units from three brigades totaling 5,000 men, but their impact of numbers lessened due to the corridor of land that allowed only one regiment at a time to navigate itself toward the target. Col. Gould Shaw volunteered his 54th Massachusetts to lead the attack, seize the ramparts, and hold out for reinforcements from the white regiments of the 6th Connecticut and the 48th New York in the wave immediately behind them. If the gap was exploited, then the remaining Union regiments would support to take the whole position. Heavy casualties in the leading regiments were expected.

At 7:45pm the bombardment stopped and the 54th Massachusetts stormed forward, the Confederate garrison rapidly leaving their protected bunker to man their positions and allow the Union troops to within 150 yards of their positions before issuing a storm of musketry, cannister and artillery fire at the ranks of blue. Taking horrendous casualties as they stormed up and onto the fort's parapets, the Union troops fought hand-to-hand with the Confederate defenders; Gould Shaw was killed instantly by musketry. The supporting Connecticut and New York regiments struggled to make headway on the 54th's western flank, and after two hours of fighting further rebel reinforcements succeeded in driving off the Union assault, capturing and killing many black troops.

Overall casualties were 1,515 men, with the Confederate commander reporting his men had buried at least 800 Union bodies. Of the 600 men who had made the charge, the 54th suffered 270 casualties, one of their number being Sgt. Lewis Douglass, son of the famous black orator Frederick Douglass. Col. Gould Shaw and the white officers from the regiment that were killed were buried alongside their men in a mass grave.

Despite the failure of the attack and the heavy casualties, the siege went on for a further 60 days before Battery Wagner surrendered. The impact of the reported heroic performance of the 54th Massachusetts galvanized Northern opinion as to the fighting effectiveness of black troops. As a result, the public radically got behind the recruiting and mustering of thousands of free blacks across the Union; by the end of the war, over 180,000 had enlisted, constituting 10 percent of the Federal armed forces by 1865.

LEFT Pvt., 54th Massachusetts with his 1853 Enfield rifle. The 54th fought bravely at Fort Wagner. (Peter Dennis © Osprey Publishing)

THE BATTLE OF CHICKAMAUGA
September 19–20, 1863

By August 1863, the Confederacy had been beaten badly at Gettysburg, Pennsylvania, and lost the key strategic city of Vicksburg, with Union forces now controlling the vital waterway of the Mississippi River. The Army of the Cumberland, commanded by Maj. Gen. William Rosecrans, had now pushed the Confederates almost out of Tennessee and captured the transportation railway hub in the city of Chattanooga, located next to the Tennessee River. President Jefferson Davis knew if Rosecrans was left unchecked, then the gateway to the eastern Confederacy was open for invasion, threatening its war industries in Georgia.

Though the focus in Richmond had been on Robert E. Lee's campaigning in the eastern theater, which drew the bulk of men and materiel, the time had come for the western command to be reinforced for a concerted effort to save Tennessee. The Army of Virginia would go on the defensive and free up two divisions led by Maj. Gen. James Longstreet to transfer to and serve under the command of Maj. Gen. Braxton Bragg's Army of Tennessee, bringing its strength to over 65,000 men—enough to pose a serious threat to Rosecrans' 60,000 troops.

An initial plan in mid-September to attack the individual elements of the Army of the Cumberland south of Chattanooga was poorly executed by Bragg's commanders, with an alerted Rosecrans quickly ordering his four corps to coalesce along a 20-mile line next to the west bank of Chickamauga Creek. The local, rolling terrain was covered in a wilderness of woods, vines, and brush, making clear visibility of a battle line very difficult. The name "Chickamauga" was thought to be

LEFT The 19th Tennessee Infantry file firing. Chickamauga was a decisive victory for the Confederates.
(Steve Noon © Osprey Publishing)

an old Cherokee word meaning "river of death"—apt for what was to come in the next two days.

On the 18th, the evening before the main battle, Bragg ordered an advance across the creek by the cavalry of Brig. Gen. Nathan Bedford Forrest's corps onto the Union left flank, which was met with unexpectedly strong Union resistance. Fierce fighting took place for control of a pivotal crossing point, and by sunset, the Confederates were well established to continue the attack the following day. Bragg, however, was unaware that Rosecrans' perceived weak left flank had now been reinforced by Maj. Gen. Thomas' whole corps through a forced march.

Fighting began again the following morning as the assaults by Bragg's men on the Union left flank occupied by Thomas failed to make a breakthrough.

The casualties on both sides were heavy, reminiscent of Gettysburg a few months before, with both sides remaining on the field to continue the fighting the following day.

Longstreet arrived that night with reinforcements and was informed that Bragg had now reorganized his army into two grand wings, with his fresh Virginians facing the Union left set to attack once Rosecrans' right flank came under attack from Lt. Gen. Leonidas Polk's main assault, which Bragg believed was the weakest point. Timing and communication between the wing commanders were crucial. Meanwhile, the Union troops spent valuable hours foraging for wood to construct breastworks in preparation for the attack they knew must come.

To Bragg's fury, Polk went in much later than expected, thus giving the

Union even more time to prepare. Even so, due to the nature of the rolling terrain and limited visibility, haphazard firefights broke out all along the Union left flank. As the morning attacks intensified on his left with the need for more units to be shifted to support Thomas, Rosecrans was misinformed that he had a gap in his line on the right. In hurriedly ordering units to shore up the supposed gap instead of conferring with his chief of staff, Rosecrans created an actual gap—two brigades wide—just as Longstreet's brigades charged in. In the resulting rout, one-third of the Union army, including Rosecrans himself, was driven from the field.

A complete disaster was averted when veteran Union units commanded by Maj. Gen. Thomas spontaneously rallied to create a new defensive line on Horseshoe Ridge. Despite determined Confederate assaults to finish the job, the makeshift Union line, supported with artillery, held until the end of the day. Thomas finally ordered retreat back to Chattanooga while

Bragg's men now occupied the surrounding heights, besieging the city.

Unsure of his enemy's disposition, not knowing they were now in full retreat, and fearful of the toll the two days' fighting had exacted on his army, Bragg's inaction turned a tactical triumph for the South into a strategic defeat. Against the wishes of Longstreet and Bedford Forrest to pursue and destroy what remained of the Union forces, Bragg opted to bottle up Rosecrans in the city. Bragg had lost over 18,000 men, with the Army of the Cumberland suffering 16,000 casualties.

LEFT Maj. Gen. George H. Thomas, known as "the Rock of Chickamauga" after his unyielding defense in combat there. (Richard Hook © Osprey Publishing)

RIGHT Triangular bayonets were common and used with such weapons as the M1842 .69-caliber musket. (John White © Osprey Publishing)

THE BATTLES OF LOOKOUT MOUNTAIN AND MISSIONARY RIDGE

November 24, 1863

The Chattanooga campaign began amid the ashes of the Union's disastrous defeat at Chickamauga the month before. The Army of the Cumberland had been routed and fallen back into the city where its demoralized men scavenged for food and fuel from its dejected citizens. With its crucial transportation hub, the city was strategically important for the Union's plans to control Tennessee and then use it as a springboard to invade Georgia and capture the South's second greatest city, Atlanta. If Georgia's manufacturing base could be taken, then the defeat of the Confederacy was only a matter of time.

These plans would not come to fruition if the remnants of the Army of the Cumberland were not rescued from their siege by the Army of Tennessee. The Union garrison, starving as supplies of food and fuel ran short, was in no condition to attempt a breakout. The 48,000-strong Confederates of Maj. Gen. Braxton Bragg now occupied the dramatic heights of Lookout Mountain and Missionary Ridge overlooking the city, their artillery trained on all routes in and out. To take the city by assault would be too costly, and Bragg had too few men to attempt to cross the Tennessee River upstream and encircle it completely, so he settled instead to wait in his positions and starve them out.

Inside Chattanooga, Rosecrans proved incapable of command as his nerves betrayed him, much to the chagrin of his officers, the War Department in

LEFT Four divisions from Thomas's IV Corps storm up Missionary Ridge. (Adam Hook © Osprey Publishing)

Washington, and President Lincoln himself. Lincoln knew the situation needed saving in terms of supplying more troops, supplies, and installing a new commander who could use them properly. Fresh from his stunning success in capturing Vicksburg, Lt. Gen. Ulysses S. Grant was given command of all Union forces and dispatched to win back Tennessee at the head of the Mississippi Military Division. His objectives were clear: hold Chattanooga, reopen its supply lines to allow the reinforcements to arrive safely, clear the Confederates from their positions above the city, and finally, destroy Bragg's Army of Tennessee.

Upon his arrival, Grant immediately replaced Rosecrans with the more resolute Maj. Gen. Thomas, ordering him to hold the city at all costs while he put into operation his plan to break the siege, focusing initially on his supply problems.

He knew bringing in supplies by rail was impossible while the rebels' artillery held the high ground, so he ordered his troops to seize Lookout Valley, which lay between the Confederate positions but was shielded from them by rolling hills, allowing a wagon train to safely travel undetected into Chattanooga. Linking this route with two ferry crossing points, Grant ordered pontoons to be constructed to carry supplies to speed up the time it would take. With the "Cracker Line" (as it became known) in place by the end of October, supplies now flooded in, giving Grant the edge over Bragg in men and materiel. He was ready to go on the offensive.

On November 23, Grant gained crucial information from rebel deserters that Bragg was withdrawing some of his brigades, surmising he would try to link up with Gen. James Longstreet's army operating near Knoxville. In an effort to prevent this, Grant sent 14,000 of the 78,000 Union troops he commanded to capture a rear-guard of 600 Confederates at Orchard Knob, where Grant then established his headquarters for the remainder of the battle. On the 24th, three divisions of Gen. Joseph Hooker attacked the Confederate left flank atop Lookout Mountain, his troops fighting through the fog as they drove off the rebels, who withdrew to reinforce Missionary Ridge.

The next day, Grant ordered a coordinated, three-pronged attack on Missionary Ridge itself, with Hooker's men advancing from the south while Maj. Gen. William T. Sherman's divisions tackled the northern end and Thomas' Army of the Cumberland pinned down Bragg's center. Sherman's initial success was repulsed by a Confederate counterattack, but Hooker's men on the left of the ridge gained the rebel positions. Thomas then advanced against Bragg's weakened center in order to alleviate the pressure on Sherman's troops. However, without orders, Thomas' men took it upon themselves to not only capture the rebel positions at the base of Missionary Ridge but to charge up and over the ridge itself, successfully overrunning its 9,000 defenders. Bragg by now had scant reserves to save his position and was forced to order a retreat. The siege of Chattanooga was lifted, and Grant would now be free to order Sherman to march south on his Atlanta campaign.

RIGHT The Headquarters flag, IV Corps. The unit distinguished itself at Missionary Ridge. (Rick Scollins © Osprey Publishing)

LEFT A Confederate 1st Sgt, during the Chattanooga campaign. (Richard Hook © Osprey Publishing)

THE BATTLE OF OKOLONA

February 22, 1864

With the victory of Union forces in the Chattanooga campaign, Tennessee, in July 1863, the newly promoted Maj. Gen. U.S. Grant was now determined to capture the Mississippi state capital of Jackson. Leading 50,000 men of the Army of the Tennessee, Maj. Gen. William Tecumseh Sherman besieged the remnants of the Confederate Army of the West commanded by Gen. Joseph E. Johnston in Jackson, who would withdraw his men rather than risk capture, leaving control of central Mississippi to the Union. Grant now ordered Sherman to continue the pursuit of rebel forces and to capture the railway hub of Meridian, where the state administration was centered, as well as the state arsenal and a military prisoner-of-war stockade.

LEFT A clash between Union and Confederate cavalrymen. (Adam Hook © Osprey Publishing)

When he departed Vicksburg with 20,000 men on February 3, Sherman hoped not only to capture the town, but to push on into Alabama as far as Mobile if practicable and leave in his wake a trail of destruction in the interior. He had dispatched orders the day before for the 7,000 Union cavalry under the command of Brig. Gen. William Sooy Smith, stationed in Memphis, to rendezvous with him at Meridian, traveling via Okolona, Mississippi, and along the Mobile and Ohio Railroad by February 10. Both Smith's and Sherman's commands coordinated with a series of feints planned by Sherman to conceal his real target and divert attention from enemy forces along the intended route.

Finally recognizing the threat, Richmond's War Department issued orders for the local commander, Lt. Gen. Leonidas Polk, to converge the scant forces available to him to stop Sherman's march. Polk demurred and instead ordered the evacuation of

Meridian two days before Sherman's column arrived on February 12, destroying railway stock in and around the town. Sherman was still expecting the arrival of Smith's horse to swell his numbers and allow him to continue his march toward Alabama.

Smith, however, mysteriously delayed his departure for ten days until February 11, as his troops rode slowly, unopposed through the muddy roads of the countryside, destroying railway lines, telegraph cables, burning crops and barns, and also freeing 1,000 slaves. By February 20, Smith was still over 90 miles away, leaving a frustrated Sherman to reluctantly head back to Vicksburg. When news of this reached Smith, he ordered a halt and headed for Okolona. With his column traveling between Prairie Station and West Point, they clashed with forward units of the 2,500 Confederate cavalry of Brig.

Gen. Nathan Bedford Forrest, arguably the finest cavalry commander of the Civil War.

On February 21, concerned about the size of the enemy he faced and fearing the fate of the slaves he had just freed, Smith ordered a withdrawal back to Okolona. Bedford Forrest, though outnumbered, was eager to chase down his retreating enemy. A brigade under the command of his younger brother, Col. Jeffrey Forrest, skirmished with Smith's rear units, slowing down his march as he retreated toward Okolona itself.

Forrest Senior arrived with his main column at dawn and immediately led the first attack across the prairie south of Okolona itself. The Union horsemen had by now dismounted and constructed a series of barricades to shelter behind as the Southern cavalry attacked their front, while other units probed around Smith's flanks to find a weakness in his line. Once established, a gap was exploited until Smith was forced to order a speedy withdrawal, leaving several cannons for the rebels to capture as they hastened to establish a new defensive line on a nearby ridge. The rebels quickly attacked again, with Forrest's younger brother being killed in the first wave. The Confederates kept up the momentum all day, driving Smith's command from one defensive position to another, until only a lack of ammunition prevented Forrest inflicting more Union casualties.

By now, Smith was content to escape back to the safety of the Tennessee border, arriving on February 26. He had lost over 380 men killed, wounded or captured, and failed to support Sherman's campaign, for which he was severely reprimanded; with failing nerves, he would leave the military in September 1864.

The destruction Sherman wrought on Southern infrastructure in his Meridian campaign would be a precursor of what he would do with a much larger force on his "March to the Sea" through Georgia that November. As for Bedford Forrest, his reputation as a brilliant guerrilla leader of horse was now firmly established in the minds of Union forces, who would see him as a major threat to their lines of communications until the end of the war.

ABOVE Stamped brass cavalry officer's badge, officer's and NCO's belt buckle and a dragoon tunic button.
(Richard Hook © Osprey Publishing)

LEFT 1st Lt., 2nd Regiment South Carolina Rifles, 1864.
(Ron Volstad © Osprey Publishing)

THE BATTLE OF THE WILDERNESS
May 5–7, 1864

By May of 1864, President Lincoln had worked his way through a string of Union commanders who had failed the test of beating Robert E. Lee's Army of Northern Virginia and capturing Richmond. Unless the South's premier commander could be beaten decisively, and his army destroyed, the outcome of the Civil War was still in jeopardy. In March, Lincoln settled upon Ulysses S. Grant as his new leader of all Union armies, handing him control of over 500,000 troops stationed across the various theaters of war in the continent.

As supreme commander, he now unveiled to Lincoln his strategy that would bring about the conquest of the South—a simultaneous five-pronged offensive on strategic points across Confederate territory meant to overwhelm local enemy forces and deny the Southern leadership from reinforcing through their interior lines any breakthroughs. The new commander in the western theater, Sherman, would march into Georgia to capture Atlanta, while three other separate armies from the south, southeast, and north would occupy the Shenandoah Valley. Grant would accompany the fifth offensive—the Army of the Potomac led by Maj. Gen. George Meade—aimed at Lee's Army of Northern Virginia. Though Meade, the victor of Gettysburg the previous year, was notionally in command, it would be Grant who directed the strategy to wage a war of attrition that would ultimately bring the South to its knees in what would be called his "Overland Campaign."

All five Union armies would be on the move by May 4 with the 100,000 men of the Army of the Potomac

LEFT Lt. Gen. Grant's successful attack at the "Bloody Angle" at Spotsylvania, following the Battle of the Wilderness. (Peter Dennis © Osprey Publishing)

crossing the Rapidan River, where it was hoped a rapid advance through what was called "the Wilderness"—a wide area of dense shrubs and trees, and where Lee had won his startling victory at nearby Chancellorsville the year before. Meade's task was to attack Lee's isolated right flank before he could gather his whole army to meet the coming threat. Lee, however, was expecting a Union advance and had been preparing his forces, consisting of 60,000 troops, to move into position once he knew what Grant's objective was. Aware he was heavily outnumbered, Lee knew his best chance of victory was to bottle up Union forces in the tight spaces of the Wilderness, reduce their numerical superiority, and inflict maximum casualties with the hope that such losses would turn public opinion in the North toward a peace settlement.

Grant outlined his own plan to his commanders. Two arterial roads ran parallel toward the enemy positions from Union positions east to west: the Orange Turnpike and the Orange Plank Road. His troops were to occupy a line running between the roads and, wherever they encountered Confederate troops, attack them. On the morning of May 5, Meade sent in one corps of infantry to attack the Confederate 2nd Corps of Lt. Gen. Richard S. Ewell they now knew to be in position on the Orange Turnpike. The fighting was intense and confused, as both sides struggled with the terrain and the restriction of sight and movement as attack and counterattack went in.

By the afternoon, fighting had broken out on the Orange Plank Road, too, as the Confederate 3rd Corps encountered two Union corps. Again, the fighting was inconclusive but bloody as multiple small skirmishes erupted in the dense woodland, leaving scores of wounded on the ground with little chance of recovery. The scenes of carnage were made more horrific when sparks from the muzzles of rifles and cannon fire ignited the dry undergrowth, creating bush fires that raged out of control as night fell, consuming everything in their path, including the wounded.

Though no breakthrough had occurred, Grant was intent on maintaining the pressure the next morning and ordered Maj. Gen. Winfield S. Hancock's II Corps to again attack along the Plank Road, driving the

Confederates back and threatening the collapse of Lee's right flank. The situation was saved by the arrival and counterattack of Lt. Gen. James Longstreet's corps, which looked to have won the day until he and his staff were caught in crossfire as they sought to scout forward positions for another attack. Longstreet survived but was now out of action as the lines again became confused and both sides drew back to take stock. By dusk both sides had fought to a standstill, with thousands of wounded littering the field.

Despite taking awful losses, Grant refused to yield the momentum, ordering his columns to march southeast to flank the Confederate positions to interpose his army between Lee and Richmond. Anticipating the move, Lee had already ordered his army to relocate to new positions for the next battle in the campaign at Spotsylvania Courthouse.

RIGHT Maj. Gen. Winfield S. Hancock commanded II Corps during the battle. (Richard Hook © Osprey Publishing)

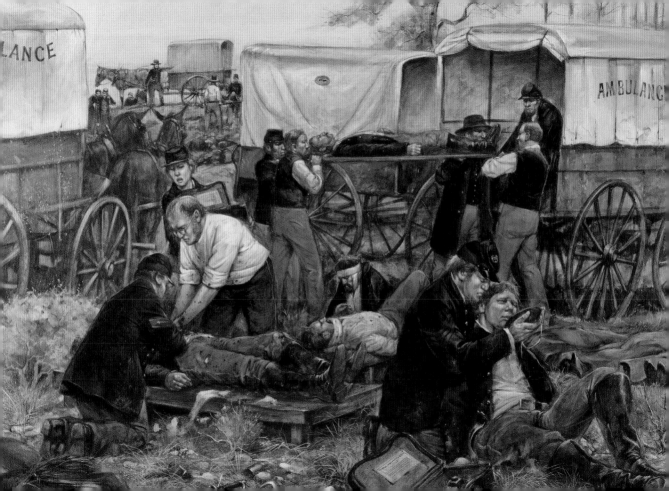

THE BATTLE OF COLD HARBOR
May 31–June 12, 1864

By the end of May, Lt. Gen. Ulysses S. Grant's Army of the Potomac was a month into fighting its war of attrition to destroy Gen. Robert E. Lee's Army of Northern Virginia. Grant's "Overland Campaign" was intent on steadfastly attempting to outflank Lee's troops in order to capture the Confederate capital Richmond, with the purpose of bringing Lee into open battle and inevitable defeat through overwhelming force of numbers and supplies. Grant, by the month's end, had suffered over 40,000 casualties as he battered the numerous entrenchments Lee used to protect his own army and inflict maximum casualties on the Union forces. The South's goal was ultimately to make the Northern public grow so tired of the struggle that they would come to the negotiating table. However, Grant was a different commander from any other Union general Lee had faced thus far, and he would continue on his grim path despite the losses suffered to achieve his strategic goal. At Cold Harbor he would learn his harshest lesson.

The crossroads of Cold Harbor lay just 10 miles north of Richmond. The area had seen bitter fighting two years previously, when Lee had driven back the same army then led by George McClellan in the Seven Days battles. As part of Grant's continuing efforts to exploit weaknesses in the Confederate right flank, Northern cavalry led by Maj. Gen. Philip Sheridan now moved on May 31 to occupy and hold the crossroads, which would allow Grant to bring up reinforcements by riverboat, and the multiple routes would allow him to either move on Richmond or attack Lee. For his part, the Confederate commander

LEFT A Federal casualty station soon after the debacle at Cold Harbor. (Richard Hook © Osprey Publishing)

was aware of the danger and surmised it must be retaken.

The next day, Sheridan's men battled to hold off concerted massed Southern infantry attacks, his cavalry troopers meeting the frontal assaults with the added firepower of their Spencer repeating carbines, inflicting heavy losses on the onrushing rebels. In the meantime, Grant rushed up infantry reinforcements to bolster Sheridan's position, with a potential Union breakthrough that afternoon only being repulsed by Lee's rapid order for fresh Confederate brigades to plug the hole that was developing. The 4,000 casualties on both sides were nothing to what was coming. That night and the following day, both sides brought up more fresh troops and established their lines adjacent to the crossroads and beyond, Grant's commanders

watching with dread as the Confederates constructed formidable earthworks to defend their positions.

Union corps and divisional commanders were aghast when they received Grant's order for a full-scale frontal assault of the Confederate line on June 3. Although Grant had directed Meade to ensure his commanders had reconnoitered the ground themselves, he had been lax in following this through. As a result, many were confused as to their objectives as well as the danger of crossing open fields toward Lee's line, where his men and artillery were protected by intricate earthworks and enjoyed a clear field of fire for anyone brazen enough to approach. The night before the attack, many Union infantrymen wove nametags onto the back of their tunics just so their bodies could later be identified, such was their certainty that the assault was doomed to fail.

At 4:30am the attack went in along the length of the line as three Union corps advanced under the cover of the morning mist to be met by withering artillery and rifle fire. In 20 minutes, over 7,000 Union men fell, a murderous repetition of the debacle Maj. Gen. Ambrose Burnside had overseen at Fredericksburg two years earlier. As more lines of infantry attempted to cross the open ground, those that had fallen in the first wave were frantically using their bayonets and canteen mugs to try to dig pits to hide from the shells landing all around them. Hundreds of wounded littered the ground. Meade was talked out of a further assault by his corps commanders who had witnessed the butchery, and by midday Grant called off the operation.

Lee's army had gotten off mildly, with only 1,500 casualties, but he was still heavily outnumbered and knew Grant would not break off the fight and retreat as his predecessors would have done. Both armies dug in and faced one another for the next nine days, the only fighting being sharp outbreaks of rifle fire between isolated units, while the dead and wounded were eventually cleared from the battlefield. Grant now decided to withdraw stealthily and again push past Lee's right flank, crossing the James River to the southeast and sweeping behind to attempt the capture of Petersburg, a vital supply hub south of Richmond. Cold Harbor would be the final large-scale battle Robert E. Lee would fight.

LEFT Sgt., 3rd New Jersey Cavalry, 1864. The unit served at Cold Harbor. (Richard Hook © Osprey Publishing)

ABOVE Flag of the 49th Georgia Infantry Regiment, which fought at Cold Harbor. (Rick Scollins © Osprey Publishing)

THE BATTLE OF KENNESAW MOUNTAIN

June 27, 1864

To many military strategists and politicians in the South in 1864, after the defeat of the Army of Northern Virginia at Gettysburg the previous summer, the ambition to invade the North in order to force a peace settlement was now abandoned. What replaced it was a desire to maintain the military ability to contest and hold what Southern territory they had and beat off sustained Federal attacks, whether in the eastern or western theaters. It would become a war of attrition that perhaps might inflict such casualties for the North that public opinion might force Washington to potentially seek an armistice. For this to have any

chance of success, the two key targets for the Union—Richmond, Virginia and Atlanta, Georgia—had to be beaten off, at the very least until the upcoming U.S. elections that November when Lincoln might well be defeated. If either city fell before that, then the Confederacy was most likely doomed.

In what would be later titled the "Atlanta campaign," Maj. Gen. William T. Sherman would lead his three armies of the Cumberland, Tennessee, and Ohio into Georgia to capture the city, with the intention of bringing the main Confederate Army of Tennessee led by Maj. Gen. Joseph E. Johnston to battle. Faced with an overwhelming superiority in men and supplies, Johnston was fully aware that the Union forces could beat his army on the battlefield; the skill was to make a successful fighting retreat to keep them away from

LEFT Union troops attack the "Dead Angle" on Pigeon Hill, where the battle was at its fiercest, and are bloodily repulsed. (Steve Noon © Osprey Publishing)

Atlanta and hope a tactical opportunity might arise to inflict enough casualties to stall their advance.

Sherman, for his part, was eager not to waste his men's lives by throwing them against layers of prepared Confederate defenses. Sherman's forces instead had opted to outflank them with sweeping maneuvers. For over 70 miles throughout May and most of June, Johnston's army was compelled to give up valuable ground as it faced encirclement from Union thrusts to both its flanks until it had reached the last natural obstacle before Atlanta—Kennesaw Mountain. It was here, with no flanking options left, and despite the formidable Confederate lines to his army's front, that Sherman decided to finally order a frontal assault. He believed it the best option to break the Confederates lines, which by now were

stretched too thin along an 8-mile line. For the main attack—on what would be later named "Cheetham Hill"—to succeed, he would order two flank attacks: on Pigeon Hill to the north and Olley's Creek, to draw enemy strength away from their center where the main Union blow would fall. If he broke this line, Sherman believed the destruction of Johnston's army was all but inevitable.

On the morning of June 27, a 200-gun bombardment attempted to soften up the rebel fortifications before the main attacks went in, but they failed to have the hoped-for impact, and the advancing Union brigades struggled to traverse not only high, rocky ground without any cover, but in some places knee-high swampland that thwarted any rapid movement required to attack an enemy. Intense fire from the Confederates inflicted appalling casualties as the lines of blue melted before the waves of musketry; those that managed to get to the Confederate lines were met with bloody hand-to-hand fighting before being captured or driven back. This was especially so on Pigeon Hill where the battle was at its fiercest and would be later dubbed "Dead Angle" by the troops assigned to take it, one brigade losing two consecutive commanders, all its field officers, and a third of its men.

Overall, despite suffering over 3,000 casualties that morning compared with Johnston's 1,000 killed or wounded, Sherman was still intent on launching fresh attacks. Warned he might use up his whole army if he tried this again, he instead switched his attention to the one success of the day, to the south of the Kennesaw line, where Federal units including cavalry had crossed Olley's Creek and progressed 5 miles to the rear of rebel positions. Ultimately, this would force Johnston to order a retreat once more. The Confederate army had won the day but tactically had lost the strategic goal of holding the Federals at such a strong defensive position. Sherman never made the mistake of ordering another frontal assault again. He still retained the men and materiel to achieve his objectives and would hold the initiative all the way to Atlanta, where he would defeat the Army of Tennessee led by a new commander—Gen. John Bell Hood—and capture the city on September 2.

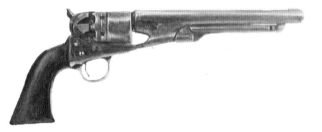

ABOVE Model 1860 .44-caliber Colt Army revolver. This weapon was widely issued to cavalrymen in the Civil War.
(Richard Hook © Osprey Publishing)

LEFT A Federal company quartermaster sergeant, cavalry, 1864.
(Ron Volstad © Osprey Publishing)

THE BATTLE OF THE CRATER— PETERSBURG

July 30, 1864

Unwilling to launch any further frontal assaults, Grant decided to surprise Lee by bypassing the prize of the Confederate capital Richmond and instead march toward Petersburg to the south. If the city were captured, then Lee's position would be untenable. The Southern general now raced to beat Grant to occupy it.

The Army of Northern Virginia, now safe behind Petersburg's trench system, easily threw back the Union assaults, and so Grant ordered his army to dig in and settle down for a siege. With overwhelming numbers of men and supplies, he knew it was only a matter of time that Lee's weakened army could hold out if their supplies were dwindling and desertions were increasing.

For a month, men of the 48th Pennsylvania Infantry, in Maj. Gen. Ambrose E. Burnside's IX Corps, had been digging a long mineshaft toward a sector of the Confederate defenses guarded by the Confederate 1st Corps. They had been miners in civilian life and their commanding officer had petitioned Burnside with an audacious plan. They would mine the secret shaft, pack it with high explosives, detonate it, destroy the enemy's defenses, and in the chaos rush through a division of Union troops to expand the hole and capture the city. Burnside discussed the plan with Meade and Grant, who, though bemused by the idea, were keen to improve the army's morale and so consented to it.

Burnside ensured the troops chosen to go in the first wave were fully trained to successfully assault, capture,

LEFT The hideous struggle in and around the Crater, July 30, 1864. (Peter Dennis © Osprey Publishing)

and then exploit the intended breach in the Confederate lines. A division of United States Colored Troops (USCT) commanded by Brig. Gen. Edward Ferrero would lead the assault and had been briefed as to the plan: two brigades would circle round their respective flanks of the explosion's crater, with one regiment exploiting the gap in the Confederate defenses, while the remainder rushed through to secure strategic positions and hold for reinforcements from the second wave of white troops who might push on to Petersburg itself.

The 500-foot-long mine shaft was completed and packed with over 7,700 pounds of explosive, sitting only 20 feet below the Confederate positions. But before the operation commenced, Meade—concerned that the Union command should not be seen to be needlessly wasting the lives of its black troops—ordered

Burnside to switch the USCT and replace them with an unprepared division of white troops from IX Corps.

On July 30 at 4:40am, the explosion blew a crater in the Confederate defenses 170 feet long, 115 feet wide and 30 feet deep, initially killing 278 defenders of the 18th and 22nd South Carolina. Delays then occurred as the Union attackers failed to adhere to Burnside's plan, with unit after unit charging into and around the crater. Hundreds of men wasted valuable time milling around in its bowel, believing it was the safest place to avoid enemy counterfire. The ensuing chaos was compounded by their own divisional commander, Brig. Gen. James H. Ledlie being absent, settling instead to get drunk behind the lines with the USCT's divisional commander Ferrero.

The Confederate position was saved by the quick thinking of the sector commander Brig. Gen. William Mahone, who, within 15 minutes of the explosion, had gathered enough men to mount a ferocious counterattack on the Union troops below. It soon developed into a one-sided "turkey shoot" as the Southerners poured a murderous rifle and artillery fire into the trapped masses below. Observing the growing disaster, Burnside decided to double down his losses and sent Ferrero's USCT division forward, who, taking on increased enemy flanking fire, rushed into the crater themselves to seek cover—only enhancing the target for the Confederates above. The chaos and slaughter increased, even when some Union troops climbed out and attempted to assault the Confederate positions, only to be forced back after several hours of fierce hand-to-hand combat. By the end of the day, IX Corps losses were staggering: 3,798 men killed, wounded or captured, the bulk of which came from the USCT division.

The siege would go on for another eight months as Grant refused further frontal assaults. Burnside, Ledlie, and Ferrero would be censured at a later board of enquiry, with Burnside's career ruined. Of the operation, Grant himself would report to Washington, "It was the saddest affair I have witnessed in this war."

LEFT Pvt., 114th Pennsylvania, Collis's Zouaves, 1864. The unit fought at Petersburg. (Bill Younghusband © Osprey Publishing)

ABOVE 13-inch siege mortar and carriage, famously used during the siege. (Tony Bryan © Osprey Publishing)

THE BATTLE OF JONESBOROUGH
August 31– September 1, 1864

By mid-July 1864, Union forces under Maj. Gen. William T. Sherman were encamped outside of Atlanta. Across the space of nine days, his combined armies of the Ohio, Cumberland, and Mississippi had dealt crushing blows to Maj. Gen. John Bell Hood's Army of Tennessee in three battles (Peachtree Creek, Atlanta, and Ezra Church). Outgunned and outnumbered, Hood, though a dogged fighter, realized he could not hold off the Union advance any longer and took his weakened army into the defenses of the city. Having seen what heavy casualties a frontal assault against entrenched works could bring, Sherman was happy to settle at the north of the city and play a waiting game. For his part, Hood was content for this to happen, believing the Union forces had overextended their supply lines and would be forced to retreat back to Chattanooga in the north sooner as a result.

Through the hot month of August, both sides monitored each other for any sign of major activity. To maintain his men's morale, Sherman was keen to keep up sporadic sorties into Southern lines as well as attack and destroy sections of the only railway link that maintained supplies, which the Confederates would then quickly repair. Sherman knew the key to the defense of Atlanta was the single railroad left running out of the city—the Macon and Western Central Railroad—which served as Hood's lifeline for his army and for the city's inhabitants. Five miles south of Atlanta itself, the Montgomery and West Point Railroad split from the Macon Railroad and headed southwest. The Northern press made capital on the stalemate it could see with Sherman and with his

LEFT Union troops begin the destruction of the railway line into Atlanta. (Richard Hook © Osprey Publishing)

commanding officer, Lt. Gen. Ulysses S. Grant, besieging Robert E. Lee's Army of Northern Virginia in Petersburg. While Grant's forces were indeed engaged in a frustrating and lengthy siege, in the west Sherman was busy devising a plan to draw Hood out of his entrenchments and destroy him.

On the morning of August 26, the troops and civilians of Atlanta awoke to see that their besiegers had vanished, with Confederate cavalry reporting to Hood only one Union Army corps remained north of Atlanta, guarding the railroad bridge over the Chattahoochee River.

Hood badly misjudged Sherman's intentions. Instead of withdrawing north, Sherman had instead decided to move seven of his eight infantry corps—70,000 men, commanded by

Maj. Gens. Howard and Thomas—in a huge flanking operation to cut that remaining rail link south of Hood's defensive lines. Two days later, Howard and Thomas' troops reached the Montgomery Railroad and set about destroying it, catching a disbelieving Hood off-guard, who convinced himself this was only a diversion from whatever main attack would come from the north.

With more reports coming in of the damage being wrought by enemy troops along his only supply route, Hood was compelled on the evening of August 30 to order Lt. Gen. William J. Hardee down the railroad to Jonesborough in an attempt to secure control of the strategically vital railroad. The following two days would be the culmination of the drawn-out Atlanta campaign.

Hardee's two corps of 24,000 men launched a series of assaults on the Union right flank, by now dug in by the river running along to Jonesborough. Intending to roll up the Union flank, the Confederate assaults failed to make any impact, with the situation deteriorating further as more reinforcements from Sherman reached the Macon Railroad further north at the town of Rough and Ready. With heavy casualties in both his corps, Hardee realized he faced far more enemy troops than he could handle and was in danger of being overwhelmed himself. Though teetering on the verge of a complete rout, through careful husbandry of feeding his final reserves into the escalating battle to shore up his flanks, Hardee managed to hold on until dusk brought respite and he could order a withdraw back toward Hood's lines.

Hood could now see for himself that Sherman's main thrust was here to sever Atlanta's remaining supply link, and if taken, it would be impossible to defend, and he would have to withdraw or risk being cut off himself. On the night of September 1, his army slipped away from their entrenchments, leaving the single corps Sherman had left behind to the north to march unopposed into Atlanta the next day. By September 2, news had reached Sherman himself, just as the newspapers across the Federal states were celebrating his spectacular victory. The capture of Atlanta would be the springboard for not only Lincoln's victory in the coming elections, but also for Sherman to now take the war to the heart of the Confederacy in Georgia.

LEFT Pvt., 1st Ohio. This trooper typifies the rugged western Yankees who entered service as "horse soldiers." (Richard Hook © Osprey Publishing)

RIGHT The Headquarters flag, XV Corps. The unit served at Jonesborough. (Rick Scollins © Osprey Publishing)

THE BATTLE OF CEDAR CREEK

October 19, 1864

As the Civil War entered its third year, Lt. Gen. Ulysses S. Grant's overall strategy to defeat the South would be through conquest and a policy of "scorched earth," destroying the South's means to fight on. Grant embraced the concept of "total war" and had devised campaigns for both the eastern and western theaters. Maj. Gen. William T. Sherman would create havoc through the heart of the Confederacy on his "March to the Sea," and in the breadbasket of northern Virginia, Maj. Gen. Franz Sigel was to sweep through the Shenandoah Valley. However, Sigel's stuttering performance against weaker opponents, and the appearance of a new formation dispatched by Robert E. Lee—the Army of the Valley—led to a change of tactics by Washington.

LEFT A Union cavalry charge against Confederate infantry, 1864. (Steve Noon © Osprey Publishing)

The new Confederate formation of 22,000 men was Lee's old 2nd Corps from the Army of Northern Virginia, and commanded by Lt. Gen. Jubal Early, a veteran of the eastern theater. It would prove to be the last Confederate invasion of the North, which like others before it traversed up through the roads of the Shenandoah toward Pennsylvania and Maryland.

Although hungry and poorly equipped, Early's forces were ordered to stay active, progress toward Washington, and distract Grant to dilute his army surrounding Petersburg to defend Washington. A Confederate force reported to be close to the capital had already sent the local population into a stir of anxiety. Grant allocated more forces to track down Early's columns, engage them, and slow his route of march, which they did, buying time for Washington's defensive works to be improved and manned with more troops. But the threat of Early still at large needed to be stamped out once and for all, and so Grant turned to a man who was as ruthless in battle as he was—his commander of cavalry for the Army of the Potomac, Maj. Gen. Philip H. Sheridan.

Through September and October, Sheridan's 32,000-man Army of the Shenandoah won victories over Early's increasingly demoralized rag-tag army at Opequon and Waynesboro. Satisfied their quarry was now on the retreat, the Union army began the systematic destruction of a 75-mile swath of the Shenandoah Valley, burning barns, crops, wagons, and farm machinery to cripple the local agricultural economy. Confident the campaign was coming to an end, Sheridan camped his forces north of Cedar Creek before traveling to Washington, D.C. for new orders.

His army reduced now to 14,000 men, Early and his commanders devised a daring plan to seize the initiative and destroy Union forces in camp with the hope of actually capturing Sheridan himself, unaware that he had departed. Ordering an all-night march along the base of the valley—in some places his men marching single file and fording two river crossings— Early's men advanced out of a dense fog in the pre-dawn hours of October 19 to catch the Federals completely unawares.

The Confederate assault overran one Union corps after another as their lines collapsed and drove past the Belle Grove Plantation. The Union VI Corps, furthest away from the line of attack, was able to offer stiffer resistance, making a determined stand for over a crucial hour behind hastily erected stone barricades in the Middletown cemetery. Nevertheless, a stunned Union army was in full retreat by 10am.

At this critical hour, Early lost his focus. Believing he had his enemy where he wanted him and ignoring the urgings of subordinate officers to press the assault and achieve total destruction of the enemy forces, he sought instead to secure captured Union cannon and prisoners, while his soldiers solidified their final line just north of Middletown. Fatally for the Southerners, exhaustion, combined with men falling out to loot the captured Union encampments, severely reduced their already small number. By now only a mile separated the two armies.

As the rebels pillaged the Union tents, Sheridan

came galloping back from Winchester with a retinue of 300 cavalrymen, unaware of the true picture of the morning's disaster, believing the sound of distant artillery was a local skirmish. Upon hearing the growing sounds of battle and streams of his men passing before him, he rode hard to the field, rallying his defeated forces, who, turning back, chanted his name. He wheeled back in his saddle and shouted, "Goddam you, don't cheer me, fight!" He then ordered his revitalized troops to re-form their lines and counterattack in force to sweep the distracted Confederates from the field.

Early's army was shattered, and the Union now owned the Shenandoah Valley. The victory gave the Northern public a morale boost and helped Lincoln achieve a landslide presidential victory three weeks later.

RIGHT Pvt., 2nd Virginia Cavalry. The Confederate unit served at Cedar Creek. (Peter Dennis © Osprey Publishing)

THE BATTLE OF NASHVILLE
December 15–16, 1864

The Civil War in the west was to come to a bloody and final climax with the devasting defeat of the Army of Tennessee led by Maj. Gen. John Bell Hood at the hands of Maj. Gen. William T. Sherman's Army of the Mississippi. Fresh from the fall of the key Confederate stronghold of Atlanta and pushing on into the Confederate heartlands, a desperate leadership in Richmond decided to back the belligerent Hood's final throw of the dice and go for broke with an all-out attack on Union forces led by Maj. Gen. George H. Thomas. It would be one of the heaviest defeats for the Confederacy and effectively hand total control of the western theater to the Union and pave the way for total victory the following year.

LEFT Maj. Gen. Nathan Bedford Forrest led the Confederate rear guard at Nashville. (Adam Hook © Osprey Publishing)

Sherman was ordered to march through the heart of the South all the way to Savannah on the Carolina coast, and "make Georgia howl," as he put it. In taking the war to the civilian population and destroying the South's manufacturing infrastructure, he intended to break their will to fight on. Realizing the Confederacy's lack of military resources to stop him, Hood proposed a plan to distract Sherman by taking what was left of his army north to invade Tennessee and capture the major Union supply base at the state's capital of Nashville.

Sherman was too focused on his own campaign, believing a mix of garrison troops stationed across Tennessee and Georgia, reinforced with three corps remaining near Atlanta, would be sufficient to thwart any move by the Confederates. The Union Army of the Cumberland would be led by the hero of Chickamauga, Maj. Gen. George H. Thomas, a contrast to Hood in tactics and leadership and who outnumbered him two to one in men.

Hood would combine his force with the cavalry corps of Maj. Gen. Nathan Bedford Forrest and with 39,000 men march into Tennessee heading toward Nashville, intending to draw out Thomas from his defensive works to fight on ground of Hood's choosing before all Union forces combined to overwhelm him. Poor operational orders allowed XIII Corps from the Army of the Ohio, led by Maj. Gen. John Schofield, to escape Hood's intended trap at the Battle of Spring Hill, 30 miles south of Nashville on November 29. The next day, determined to prevent Schofield linking with Thomas, Hood sent in waves of fruitless assaults against the defensive works Schofield's men

constructed at Franklin, 12 miles north of Spring Hill. It was a disaster, with 12 Confederate generals, 50 regimental commanders, and over 7,000 men killed or wounded, made worse as Schofield withdrew to link up with Thomas in Nashville.

Reaching Nashville on December 2, Hood's depleted army took up defensive redoubts along a 4-mile line south of the city, with the intent of fighting off a Union assault. Thomas spent the next two weeks assessing the Southern positions before he struck. Pinning down Hood's right flank with a weaker force, he sent in overwhelming numbers to strike his right and take the redoubt system. The Federals drove the Southerners back after fierce fighting to a new defensive line, two hills—Shy's Hill to the west and Overton Hill to the east—linked by a stone wall and entrenchments. Again, Thomas employed the successful tactic of the previous day, a heavy Union artillery barrage softening up Confederate positions as massed infantry hit Hood's right flank, forcing him to draw off troops from other positions. As a result, these positions were poorly manned for the final assault on his left, which broke under intense pressure by the late afternoon.

The defeat at Nashville, the last major battle of the Civil War, marked the end of Hood's career and the destruction of the Army of Tennessee, which had lost over 50 percent of its strength. The victory for the Union now freed up Sherman to focus fully on bringing Georgia to its knees and bring ultimate victory over the Confederacy one step closer.

LEFT Gen. John Bell Hood, commander of the Army of Tennessee. (Richard Hook © Osprey Publishing)

RIGHT Southern-made J.P. Murray muzzle-loading carbine attached to a sling with an iron hook. (Gerry Embleton © Osprey Publishing)

THE BATTLE OF BENTONVILLE
March 19–21, 1865

This would be the last major confrontation between the Union and Confederacy in the western theater. Fresh from his victorious "March to the Sea," which had gutted the heart of Georgia, Maj. Gen. William T. Sherman now led his Army of the Mississippi north into the Carolinas, intending to meet with Ulysses S. Grant in Virginia. Sherman had split his forces in two—the left wing (the Army of Georgia) commanded by Maj. Gen. Henry W. Slocum, and the right wing (the Army of the Tennessee) led by Maj. Gen. Oliver O. Howard—as they marched north independently, destroying rebel supplies and rail lines in their path until they rendezvoused at Goldsboro, North Carolina.

LEFT Confederate sharpshooters firing at advancing Northern troops. (Johnny Shumate © Osprey Publishing)

Robert E. Lee ordered Gen. Joseph E. Johnston to command the only Southern force in the vicinity and to gather together whatever other units he could muster to block their progress. Combining the remnants of the Army of Tennessee, units from Lee's own Army of Northern Virginia, and troops from Georgia, Florida, and South Carolina, Johnston morphed them into a new command—the Army of the South. Outnumbered three to one, he thought if the Confederates could isolate and attack Slocum's wing at Bentonville before it could combine with Howard's, then they stood a chance. Unfortunately, the maps Johnston's staff were using prior to the battle incorrectly placed the wings a greater distance from one another than they were, which would have consequences for Johnston over the coming days.

The Army of the South established a defensive line 1 mile outside of Bentonville along the main road running north and awaited Slocum's arrival as they marched toward Goldsboro. Advancing toward what he believed to be nominal enemy resistance, Slocum underestimated its size, with his initial orders to disperse them using a single infantry division failing as the battle quickly escalated.

Bringing up his whole wing took some time, as Johnston's forces now pressed forward along the frontline. Sending word to Howard and Sherman bringing up reinforcements 12 miles further behind him, Slocum ordered his divisional commanders to establish a linear line of defense, but crucially not to construct breastworks. As the day progressed, it dawned on Slocum that he was facing a whole Confederate army.

By 3pm, the Army of the South was in position and now attacked the

Federals in strength, Confederate infantry crashing into Slocum's left flank, driving them back and capturing many prisoners, including a corps field hospital. As the rebels gained ground on the flanks, various divisions were now being enfiladed by Southern fire as the Union line started to buckle, a situation almost repeated on the Union right, too. A complete disaster was averted only by a lack of coordination as the Confederates assaulted the Union front and its center, holding them before successfully counterattacking. The fighting continued sporadically until midnight, when the Confederates withdrew to their start lines and began to dig in.

The following afternoon, Slocum received the first batch of fresh troops from Howard's wing now arriving piecemeal onto the battlefield, who extended his right flank and allowed him to reinforce weaker areas. Johnston was now facing the combined strength of Union forces he feared, but aware his army was all that stood in the way of Sherman continuing into Virginia, he ordered his men to hold their ground for as long as practicable. He held the vain hope that an impatient Sherman might resort to wasteful infantry assaults against his established defensive positions—thus evening out the odds. Having learned to his detriment outside of Atlanta how costly this option would be, Sherman was content to simply send in skirmishers to probe the enemy lines.

On March 21, a localized reconnaissance by Union forces on their right flank developed into a major assault by two whole brigades that exploited gaps in the Confederate line, threatening the whole Southern defense and sealing off any chance Johnston might have to retreat back across the bridge over Mill Creek, which anchored his whole position. Early success had

the Union brigades only 1 mile away from the crossing until a timely counterattack of Southern cavalry and an order from Sherman himself called a halt to the attack, saving the situation for Johnston. That night he ordered the Army of the South to quietly pull back from their positions, burning the bridge as they left but still leaving the route north open for Sherman to now exploit.

RIGHT Flag of the 1st Tennessee Infantry, which fought at Bentonville. (Rick Scollins © Osprey Publishing)

LEFT Maj. Gen. William T. Sherman commanded the Army of the Mississippi at Bentonville. (Richard Hook © Osprey Publishing)

THE BATTLE OF APPOMATTOX COURT HOUSE

April 9, 1865

After its bloody advance through the Wilderness in Lt. Gen. Ulysses S. Grant's "Overland Campaign," the Army of the Potomac had since spent nine long months besieging the city of Petersburg. The well-supplied Union forces numbered over 125,000 men as they sat out the siege in their entrenchments stretching over 50 miles in length, which cut the city off from any hope of reinforcement. Inside the city, the remnants of Gen. Robert E. Lee's once glorious Army of Northern Virginia sat behind their defensive works, ill equipped, ragged, and starving. Lee's numbers had dwindled through continuous desertions, from 60,000 to just over 35,000 men, barely enough to hold the full length of the city's defenses and certainly unable to withstand a coordinated assault from Grant's forces.

Three Union armies were now converging on Lee: Grant to his front, reinforced by Maj. Gen. Philip Sheridan's Army of the Shenandoah, while coming up from the south marched the combined strength of Maj. Gen.'s William T. Sherman and John M. Schofield. Lee well understood what this meant for his army and for Richmond should all Union forces coalesce on his position. Petersburg would fall, to be quickly followed by Richmond itself, and thus seal the destruction of the Confederacy. Only the Army of Tennessee, led by Lt. Gen. Joseph Johnston in the hills of central North Carolina, would be left to carry on the fight. By February, Lee was already making plans

LEFT The last "rebel yell"—Appomattox Court House, April 9, 1865. (Adam Hook © Osprey Publishing)

to withdraw from their precarious position and make for the west. Grant for his part was acutely aware that the Confederates might well slip away now that the winter Virginia roads were passable with the coming of better weather.

On April 1, a Confederate division was repulsed at Five Forks, just southwest of Petersburg, where a vital supply rail hub was located, and potentially an avenue for a Southern escape route. The following day, Grant ordered a general assault all along the southern front of the Petersburg line, achieving a breakthrough after fierce trench fighting and forcing Lee to abandon his positions and to send word to President Davis that he had just hours to escape via rail. As Grant's troops finally entered the city, to the west the Army of Northern Virginia

crossed the Appomattox River, heading in the direction of Lynchburg where Lee hoped to pick up much-needed supplies at Appomattox Station. Union forces were already snapping at his heels as the Southerners fought a series of running battles. At Sayler's Creek on April 6, a sudden attack by Sheridan's cavalry corps split the Confederate line and led to the capture of a quarter of Lee's remaining troops as well as eight generals, including Lee's own son Eustace. The delays caused by the fighting resulted in Lee failing to beat Sheridan in the race to Appomattox Station, where Union cavalry captured and destroyed the intended rebel supplies and blocked the Confederates' path further westwards.

By April 8, 125,00 Union troops were now encircling Lee's position, cutting off any hope of escape. The day before Grant had dispatched a note to Lee asking him to consider surrender to prevent further bloodshed, but Lee refused and instead ordered Maj. Gen. John B. Gordon to make a last-ditch attempt at breakout with his 2nd Corps at dawn the next day. An initial breakthrough of the first line of Union cavalry led Gordon's forces to crest a ridge where they viewed the dreadful sight of the entire Army of the James in order of battle ready to block them. A forlorn Gen. Lee remarked to his staff officers, "There is nothing left for me to do but to go and see Gen. Grant, and I would rather die a thousand deaths." He would sign the surrender at the McLean House at 1pm that afternoon.

Grant offered generous terms to the defeated Confederates. Lee's army was to be paroled, officers were to keep their sidearms, and enlisted men could retain their horses and mules in order to travel home and participate in spring planting of their crops. Grant also ordered Union Army rations to be delivered to Lee's starving men. On April 10, Lee gave a farewell address to his troops, who then marched off toward Union lines to stack their arms and be paroled. Famously, Brig. Gen. Lawrence Chamberlain gave the Union salute to the vanquished Confederate columns as they passed by. Four years of bloody civil war were now at an end.

LEFT The ragged Army of Northern Virginia was ill equipped for the battle. (Gerry Embleton © Osprey Publishing

RIGHT Maj. Gen. Joshua Chamberlain, who received the formal surrender of the Army of Northern Virginia on April 12. (Richard Hook © Osprey Publishing)

INDEX

Figures in **bold** refer to illustrations.